Handshake

a course in communication

Workbook ●

PETER VINEY & KAREN VINEY

Oxford University Press 1996

Oxford University Press,
Great Clarendon Street, Oxford OX2 6DP

Oxford New York
Athens Auckland Bangkok Bogota Bombay
Buenos Aires Calcutta Cape Town Dar es Salaam
Delhi Florence Hong Kong Istanbul Karachi
Kuala Lumpur Madras Madrid Melbourne
Mexico City Nairobi Paris Singapore
Taipei Tokyo Toronto

and associated companies in
Berlin Ibadan

OXFORD and OXFORD ENGLISH
are trade marks of Oxford University Press

ISBN 0 19 4572226
© Peter Viney and Karen Viney 1996

First published 1996

Acknowledgements

*The publishers would like to thank the following for permission to
reproduce photographs:*
Aquarius
Camera Press Ltd, Baron, Hugh Sibley, Mark Tillie
Bruce Coleman Ltd, John Burton
The Independent, Philip Meech, 'Waiting for the post office to open'.
The Natural History Museum, London
Stockfile, Steven Behr
Virago / Little Brown, Tom Victor

Commissioned photography by
Emily Andersen (pages 45, 72, 81)
Rob Judges (page 59, payphone)
Mark Mason (pages 17, 50, 59)

Illustrations by
Kathy Baxendale (pages 33, 60)
Gay Galsworthy (page 21, exercise 3)
Ian Kellas (pages 6, 7, 9, 10, 11, 22, 41, 42, 52, 55, 65, 73, 76, 84)
Henning Löhlein (page 21, exercise 1)
Chris Price (page 19)
Harry Venning (page 43)
Brian Walker (page 30)

*The authors and publishers would like to thank the following for
permission to use adapted material and / or reproduce copyright
material in this book:*
Hodder Headline PLC Group: extract from 'Body Language' from
Debrett's Guide to Business Etiquette by Nicholas Yapp (page 36)
A.P. Watt: extract from *Foreign Bodies* by Peter Collett (page 68)

Design by Shireen Nathoo Design

Printed in Hong Kong

Contents

Before you begin

There is a Workbook unit for each Student's Book unit. The Workbook units have three parts.

Thinking about learning

This section comes at the beginning of each Workbook unit. You can do it before the unit or at any time during the unit.

Sections

In this Workbook the section headings have the same titles as the Student's Book sections. Use each Workbook section after the Student's Book section. Remember that there is also a **Language Focus** section in the Student's Book.

After you've finished

After you've finished work on the Student's Book and Workbook unit, you can do this section. There is a **Skills check** and a **Grammar check**.

Thinking about learning

Vocabulary, grammar, and communication

We are going to use the example of requesting. When we request, we use three areas of language:
- vocabulary
- grammar
- communication skills

The first thing that we think about is vocabulary. You remember words for requesting. Then you think about grammar. It is easy to forget communication skills. Look at the chart.

using English		
vocabulary	please	to ask for
	to request	a request
	a favour	would like
	want	have
	can, could, may	I wonder
	tea, coffee, a drink, etc.	
	this, that, these, those	
grammar	Which is correct?	
	Can I have? or Do I can have?	
	Give me or Give my or Give I?	
	I'd like a tea, please or I like a tea, please?	
	Can you say:	
	May you get me a tea?	
communication	what you say	
	how you say it	
	when you say it	
	where you say it	
	why you say it	
	who you say it to	
	what you don't say	

What do *you* worry about most, vocabulary, grammar, or communication?

Grammar

Most of us worry about grammar. You either know the vocabulary or not! You can request things easily if you know the vocabulary. Just say *coffee* and smile.

Grammar is an important part of all language courses. We can think about grammar in three ways.

using English			
grammar facts	*Me* is an object pronoun.		
	Can is a modal verb.		
	The question form is *Can I... ?*		
	You can't use *May you* as a request.		
grammar patterns	I	can	do it.
	You	can't	get it.
	He	cannot	have it.
	She		
	It		
	We		
	They		
grammar choices	Is there a difference between *Can I have it?* and *Could I have it?*		
	Is there a difference between *I'd like one* and *I want one?*		

You can find more information about grammar in the Active Grammar appendix of the Student's Book.

For example, you might want to know about object pronouns. You'll see this sign in the Student's Book:

 See Active Grammar
object pronouns

Try it now. Then look at the tasks below.

1 Grammar patterns

Make a grammar pattern chart for *could / couldn't*.

2 Vocabulary lists

Look through the Student's Book quickly. Write two vocabulary lists, one for uncountable nouns, the other for countable nouns.

3 Navigating the Student's Book

Look through the Student's Book and find this information.

- In the Glossary, which word comes after *formula*? Which word comes before *formula*?
- In the Active Grammar appendix, find **determiners**. Which page are they on? What comes after **determiners**?
- In the Listening appendix, on which page is the *Room service* dialogue from the Introductory unit?
- Turn to the Language Focus section for the Introductory unit. Look at the first page. Which is the fifth example in **3**?

For the student: Asking for help

1 Basic expressions

Phrase books usually begin with a short list of basic expressions in the language. Here is a list for English.

Yes	*OK*
No	*Sorry*
Please	*Excuse me*
Thanks	*Hello*
Goodbye	*You're welcome*

You're going to teach a friend five words or expressions in English every day. Which five are you going to teach on the first day? Put a tick (✔).

Think of five more words and expressions for the third day.

2 *Excuse me / Pardon (me) / Sorry*

You can use these three expressions in several ways:
- as questions, when you don't understand or don't hear
  Pardon? Sorry?
  Pardon me? (USA) Excuse me? (USA)
  I beg your pardon? (formal)
  What? (informal, not polite)
  Use rising intonation.
- when you walk into someone in a busy place accidentally
  Sorry. Pardon me. Excuse me.
  This is an apology.
  Don't use rising intonation.
- when you want to go past someone
  Excuse me. / Excuse me, please.
  Don't use rising intonation.
- before a request, interrupting someone
  Excuse me, … Sorry, … Pardon me, …
  (USA)
  Excuse me, can I ask you something?

In conversation the three expressions are often interchangeable (you can use any of them), but the sentences above show you the main meaning.

Use the main meanings of *Excuse me*, *Pardon*, and *Sorry* to complete the speech bubbles.

1 .... , may I interrupt you?

2 ....? I don't understand.

3 .... !

4 .... That was an accident.

Conversations

Complete the spaces in this conversation.

A: I'd .... a video tape, please.

B: .... like VHS, Hi-8, or VHS-C?

A: ....

B: .... size – 240, 180, or 60?

A: I .... a three-hour tape.

B: That's an E180. What .... would you like?

A: Maxell.

B: A Maxell E-180. .... £4.99.

A: There ....

Requests

1 Informal and formal requests

Here are some requests. Someone is saying them with a polite tone of voice and intonation. Grade them from *A* (very informal) to *F* (very formal).

1 I wonder if I could have a glass of water. .....
2 Can I have an apple juice? .....
3 A hot chocolate, please. .....
4 May I have a milk shake? .....
5 Give me a cola. .....
6 Could I have an orange juice, please? .....

2 Word order

have / tea? / I / some / Could
Could I have some tea?

Rewrite these sentences in the correct order.

1 coffee. / me / a / Give
2 please? / menu / the / see /we / Could
3 another / of / May / have / glass / I / please? / water / mineral
4 wonder / tea / could / if / I / more / some / please? / have / I
5 wine. / I'd / some / like
6 please. / water / Sparkling

If you don't know the words ...

1 Demonstratives

Complete the spaces with *this, that, these,* and *those.*

1 'Is ....
   a UFO?'

2 ' .... are my
   children, Tiffany
   and Cedric.'

3 ' .... are
   polar bears.'

4 'Look, ...
   is my new watch.'

2 Food questions

Think about these questions, then write a short text about breakfast in your country.

– What's your favourite hot drink?
– What's your favourite cold drink?
– Do you have a hot drink for breakfast?
– What do you have for breakfast?
– What do most people have for breakfast in your country?

3 Pronunciation

Say these words aloud. All of them are in the Introductory unit. The underlined sounds are the same.

jam	that	ham	can
plate	Danish	may	make
What	hot	not	coffee
those	hotel	slowly	toast
cup	but	butter	uncountable
use	menu	you	two
egg	red	menu	bread
cheese	please	these	mean
this	milk	still	mineral
ice	rice	size	five

When you are working on your own, try making some pronunciation lists. Note words with the same sounds.

Room service

☛ See also **Language Focus: Quantity** for more exercises on countable and uncountable nouns.

1 Word square

Find the food and drink words in this word square. They are all words you can find on a breakfast menu.

B	S	A	S	C	R	A	M	B	L	E	D
O	A	G	O	C	R	O	L	L	P	J	S
I	U	B	T	O	M	A	T	O	E	S	T
L	S	U	O	R	A	N	G	E	A	C	R
E	A	T	F	N	N	H	A	M	R	I	A
D	G	T	M	F	R	I	E	D	H	R	W
E	E	E	U	L	M	P	J	A	M	B	B
G	B	R	E	A	D	U	J	U	I	C	E
G	L	X	S	K	T	W	T	Q	L	V	R
Y	H	E	L	E	D	Z	E	A	K	K	R
D	A	N	I	S	H	P	A	S	T	R	Y
P	O	A	C	H	E	D	B	A	C	O	N

2 Compound words

Make compound words from the list below.

orange	bread	boiled	yoghurt
sugar	pot	tea	pastries
wholewheat	juice	plain	eggs
Danish	bowl		

3 Countable or uncountable?

Complete the spaces with *is* or *are*.

1 .... there any more milk?

2 There .... some boiled eggs over there.

3 There .... some scrambled egg over here.

4 There .... some sugar in the bowl.

5 There .... some bowls of sugar on the tables.

6 Excuse me, ... there any orange juice left?

7 How many glasses .... there?

8 How much jam .... there in the pot?

4 Increase your vocabulary

Use a dictionary and this chart to answer the questions.

	egg	meat	fish	vegetables	potato(es)	rice
fried	✓	✓	✓	✓	✓	✓
boiled	✓	✓		✓	✓	✓
poached	✓		✓			
scrambled	✓					
baked		✓	✓		✓	
roast		✓	✓	✓	✓	
mashed					✓	

– Which are the most popular cooking methods in your country?
– Do you prefer fried rice or boiled rice?
– Do you prefer roast potatoes or mashed potatoes?
– Do you prefer baked fish or fried fish?
– What things can you use to poach fish? Water? Milk? Wine?
– Do you fry things in olive oil, corn oil, or a different oil?

Several words can be countable or uncountable. *Some scrambled egg, some mashed potato* or *some scrambled eggs, some mashed potatoes*. Are you thinking about the scrambled egg or mashed potato on your plate? You can't count it. Or are you thinking of the eggs and potatoes before someone scrambled or mashed them? You can count them!

Requesting for others

1 Who is it for?

Write sentences as in the example.

He'd like the fried steak.
The fried steak's for him.

1 We'd like the tomato soup.
2 She'd like the poached fish.
3 I'd like the grapefruit juice.
4 They'd like the fried chicken.
5 He'd like the scrambled egg.

2 We'd like some wine

Write sentences as in the example.

Please bring us some wine.
We'd like some wine.

1 Please show them the menu.
2 Bring me the bill.
3 Pass her the pepper, please.
4 Give him some water.
5 Can you get us some bread?

3 Contractions

We'd is a contraction for *we would* in **2** above. What do these contractions mean?

1	I'm	6	You'd like
2	He's got	7	She's busy
3	They've got	8	We're sorry
4	I don't	9	He doesn't
5	She can't	10	It's for me

Culture comparison

When you are visiting a foreign country on business or on holiday, food is one of the main topics of conversation. Read this.

> **Why do airlines always serve chicken?**
> 'Chicken again!' International airlines always serve chicken. Why? Well, some food is taboo for religious reasons. Muslims and Jews don't eat pork and Hindus don't eat beef. Then there are national traditions. For example, the British don't like snails, and never eat horsemeat. Lamb isn't very popular in the USA. The Japanese eat less dairy produce than Westerners. Some people are vegetarians (of course, they don't eat chicken either). Other people don't eat red meat for health reasons. There are also unusual foods that are only popular in one country or in one region. You can buy alligator meat in Florida, and kangaroo meat in Australia. Airlines serve chicken, not because so many people like it, but because so few people dislike it.

1 Vocabulary

Find words in the text which mean:

1 meat from pigs
2 meat from cattle
3 meat from young sheep
4 milk, cheese, butter, etc.
5 people who never eat meat
6 a slow-moving mollusc that carries its shell on its back.

2 Comprehension

Why do airlines always serve chicken?
Choose the best answer.

– There are many different methods of cooking chicken.
– Chicken is a popular international food.
– Few people have taboos against chicken.
– Chicken isn't expensive.
– Chicken is good for your health.

3 International food?

Are these words international? Do you need to translate these words into your language?

spaghetti	pizza	hamburger	hot dog
lasagne	sandwich	omelette	quiche
paella	fries	kebab	chocolate
nachos	sushi	yoghurt	

4 Food in your country

Think about these questions, then write a short text about food in your country.

– What food is typical of your region?
– What's a typical menu?
– Are there many foreign restaurants in your country?
– Is American food popular in your country?

After you've finished

Skills check

Do you think these statements are true (✔) or false (✘) for you?

1 Intonation is very important when you request something. .....
2 *Could I have ...?* is always more polite than *Can I have ...?* .....
3 Nearly all the uncountable words in English are also uncountable in my language. .....
4 Smiling and body language are not really important when you request something in English. .....
5 I'm going to think more about how I say something in English, not just the right grammar. .....

Grammar check

You can test yourself. Choose the correct word.

1 (Do / Would / May) you like a drink?
2 I'd like a mineral water, but (not / nothing / no) ice.
3 Please pass (I / me / my) the salt.
4 (Could / May / Might) you bring me some tea?
5 Four of (this / that / these), please.
6 I'd (like / liking / to like) the salad, please.
7 Can you bring (we / our / us) a menu, please?
8 The fish is for him, and the meat is for (she / her / hers).
9 'Thank you.' '(Please / You're welcome).'
10 Can you say that more (slowly / slow / not fast)?
11 How (are / does / do) you spell that?
12 Could you (to explain / explain / explaining) this word?
13 Sorry, I ('m not / not / don't) understand.
14 What (is / does / do) 'apologize' mean?
15 'Coffee, please.' 'OK, there (it / you / the coffee) go.'
16 Would you like still (and / with / or) sparkling water?
17 Can I have an (orange / oranges) juice?
18 Could you (take / have / bring) me a menu?
19 Are you (now / finished / ready) to order?
20 (I / I'm / I'd) wonder if I could see the menu, please?

Thinking about learning

How do you learn?

Think about how you learn. Don't only think about learning languages. Think about how you learn other things, too. Which of the sentences below are true for you?

1   You are assembling a new bookshelf.
    A   I read the instructions and look at the diagrams.
    B   I ask someone to tell me what to do.
    C   I assemble it without looking at the instructions.

2   You are at a lecture.
    A   I like looking at handouts, and at diagrams on the board. I write notes during the lecture.
    B   I like listening to the lecturer. I don't like making notes.
    C   I don't like sitting and listening.

3   In language lessons:
    A   Reading is my favourite activity. I like the pictures in the book.
    B   Discussion is my favourite activity. I like talking.
    C   Role-play is my favourite activity. I like doing things.

4   When I learn new words:
    A   I'm good at spelling. I 'see' the word in my mind.
    B   I'm good at pronunciation. I think of the sound of the word. I move my mouth and say the word to myself.
    C   I remember words by using them in conversation or in writing.

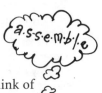

5   When I'm speaking on the phone in my own language:
    A   I speak quickly. I often 'doodle' (draw on a piece of paper).
    B   I speak at normal speed.
    C   I speak carefully. I move my hands a lot.

6   Do you listen to music while you're studying?
    A   I like listening to music while I'm studying.
    B   I can't listen to music and study at the same time.
    C   When I hear music, I want to move.

How did you answer? Turn to page 19 to find out what your learning style is.

Everyone learns by using all three learning styles, but most of us prefer one style. If you know your learning style, you can do more practice in the things you aren't so good at. If you know someone else's learning style, you will know how to present information to them. This makes you a better communicator.

Greetings

1   Greetings

Look at the greetings below. Can we reply to all of them by repeating the same expression? Write Y (yes) or N (no).

..... Good morning.
..... Good afternoon.
..... Good evening.
..... Hello.
..... How do you do.
..... Hi.

2 Vocabulary

Complete the spaces with these words.

acquaintance(s)	co-worker(s)	friend(s)
relative(s)	stranger(s)	

1 When he arrives at the office, he greets his

....

2 I like family parties. It's good to see my

.... again.

3 'He's not a close friend,' said the movie

star. 'He's only an ....'

4 I always tell my children 'Never talk to

....'

5 He's a very old .... We were at school

together.

Culture questionnaire

1 Irregular plurals of nouns

What are the singular nouns for these plurals?

1 men	3 children	5 teeth	7 sheep
2 people	4 women	6 feet	8 mice

2 Relatives

Look at the list of female relatives and friends. Write in the male equivalents. Remember that some of these do not change in English!

1 mother ....

2 grandmother ....

3 daughter ....

4 sister ....

5 sister-in-law ....

6 aunt ....

7 niece ....

8 cousin ....

9 wife ....

10 stepmother ....

11 girlfriend ....

12 partner ....

13 neighbour ....

14 colleague ....

15 friend ....

3 Mind map

If you are a visual learner, mind maps are a good way of remembering things. Complete the mind map with information about yourself.

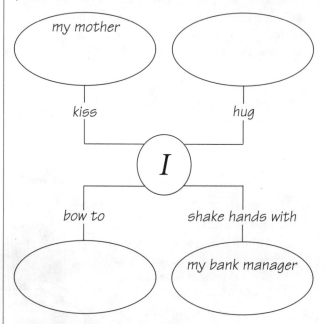

Introducing yourself

How do you want people to address you? When you introduce yourself in a formal situation, you can show people how you want them to address you.

introduction – what you say	reply
(for men)	
Hello, my name's Smith.	Hello, Mr Smith.
Hello, my name's Smith. John Smith.	Hello, Mr Smith.
Hello, my name's John. John Smith.	Hello, John.
(for women)	
Hello, my name's Smith.	Hello, Ms Smith.
Hello, my name's Smith. Mrs Smith.	Hello, Mrs Smith.
Hello, my name's Anna. Anna Smith.	Hello, Anna.

Don't say ~~My name's Mr Smith / My name's Mrs Smith.~~
Don't forget to use the same greeting words in the reply:
Hello for *Hello, Good morning* for *Good morning.*

Write replies to these introductions.

1   Hi, I'm Annette. Annette Green.
2   (A woman says) Good morning, my name's Kennedy.
3   Good afternoon, my name's Simpson. Miss Simpson.
4   Hello, my name's Wilson. Mrs Wilson.
5   (A man says) Good evening, my name's Clinton.
6   Hello, my name's Tony. Tony Blair.
7   (A woman says) Hello, my name's Redgrave.

Sometimes we don't translate well-known foreign forms of address in formal situations or when we are talking about famous people. For example: *Monsieur Chirac, Madame / Mademoiselle Lefort* (French); *Herr Schmidt, Frau / Fraulein Keller* (German); *Señor Lopez, Señora / Señorita García* (Spanish); *Signor Andreotti, Signora / Signorina Pavarotti* (Italian). We don't normally do this for other languages.

Introductions

1   Choose the correct verb

Here's some advice about introductions. Complete the spaces with one of these verbs.

| state | shake | reply | introduce |
| look | exchange | | |

1   When people meet on business, they often .... cards.
2   Women choose whether to .... hands with men or not.
3   .... younger people to older people.
4   Always .... your name clearly.
5   .... the other person straight in the eye and smile.
6   In Britain, ... 'How do you do' if the other person says 'How do you do.'

2   Complete the spaces

Complete the spaces in this conversation. You can use one word to complete all the spaces.

A: Good morning. My name's Carter. Rob Carter.

B: Pleased .... meet you, Mr Carter.

A: I'd like .... introduce my colleague. This is Carmen Peterson.

B: Hello, Ms Peterson. It's good .... meet you.

C: It's nice .... meet you, too.

B: Are you going .... be in England long?

C: No, we're going .... travel to Belgium tomorrow.

3   Verbs + infinitives with *to*

Complete the spaces using these verbs.

| stop | read | meet | get | go |
| visit | see | | | |

3214 East Orange Drive
Orlando, Florida
May 27th

Dear Gina,

I was very pleased to .... your letter last week. It was good to .... all your news.
I'd like to .... Michael. He sounds very interesting.
I'm going to .... Universal Studios tomorrow. I hope to .... on all the rides, especially 'Back To The Future'.
Well, it's time for me to .... now. I have to catch the mail. I hope to .... you in England next month.

Lots of love,

Stephanie

13

Introducing other people

1 Matching

Match the questions which mean the same.

1 What's your name? .....
2 What nationality are you? .....
3 What's your address? .....
4 What's your job? .....
5 How old are you? .....
6 What's your date of birth? .....
7 Are you married? .....

A What do you do? .....
B What's your age? .....
C When were you born? .....
D Who are you? .....
E Where do you live? .....
F Are you single? .....
G Which country do you come from? .....

Which questions do people use in friendly conversation? (write *F*)
Which questions do people use in official situations (e.g. at an airport)? (write *O*)
Of course we use some of the questions in friendly conversations and in official situations.

2 About you

Change the information in these sentences so that they are true for you.

1 My name's Julia Cooper.
2 I come from New Zealand.
3 I live in Christchurch.
4 I'm a scientist.
5 I work for Cook Chemicals.
6 I'm twenty-eight.
7 I'm single.

3 About another person

Look at exercise 2. Write a short text about someone you know.

4 Countries and nationalities

Complete this table.

	country	nationality
-ish	England	....
	Spain	....
	....	Swedish
	....	Polish
	Scotland	....
	Ireland	....
	Turkey	....
-an/-ian	Australia	....
	Canada	....
	....	Brazilian
	....	German
	United States	....
	Mexico	....
	Italy	....
-ese	....	Japanese
	China	....
	....	Vietnamese
	Portugal	....
-i	Pakistan	....
	Iraq	....
others	Netherlands	....
	France	....
	....	Swiss

5 Nationalities – spelling

There are six basic groups of nationality words:
- ending in -ish
- ending in -ian
- ending in -an
- ending in -ese
- ending in -i
- irregular (e.g. Swiss, Greek).

Can you think of more nationalities for each group?

Shaking hands

1 Word square

How many adjectives can you find in this word square? They are all from the Student's Book.

```
U  F  G  I  C  Q  A  B  K  D  F
N  E  R  V  O  U  S  X  T  Z  O
F  A  S  A  L  E  S  J  W  C  R
R  G  X  A  D  W  E  A  K  T  M
I  G  C  H  E  E  R  F  U  L  A
E  R  E  Y  W  T  T  V  G  P  L
N  E  C  O  N  F  I  D  E  N  T
D  S  S  H  Y  I  V  U  N  I  C
L  I  M  P  L  R  E  H  T  C  M
Y  V  W  A  R  M  Y  Q  L  E  O
R  E  S  T  R  O  N  G  E  Z  L
```

2 When do you shake hands?

Tick the answers that are true for you.

I shake hands:

..... when I meet someone for the first time in a formal situation.

..... when I meet someone for the first time in an informal situation.

..... when I see an old friend.

..... when I arrive at a close friend's home.

..... when I congratulate someone (after an exam, or because it's their birthday).

..... when I meet business colleagues.

..... when I leave business colleagues.

..... when I meet business acquaintances.

..... when I leave business acquaintances.

..... every time I say goodbye to people.

Re-introducing yourself

1 Conversation

Complete the spaces in the conversation.

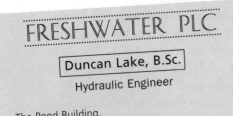

FRESHWATER PLC

Duncan Lake, B.Sc.

Hydraulic Engineer

The Pond Building,
Bradford, Yorkshire, BD8 6YW

Lancashire Water Plc

Alison Green, BA, LL B
Environmental Law Consultant

LWP Tower,
Clogthorpe, Lancashire M21 6YH

A: ....

B: Oh, hello, um, er…

A: The Chicago conference last year?

B: ....

A: My name's ....

B: ....

A: How's business?

B: ....

2 What do you say?

Imagine you're at an international conference. What do you do in these situations? Choose an answer.

1 A complete stranger says, 'Hello! Great to see you!' What do you do?
   A Say, 'Sorry. Do I know you?'
   B Smile, say, 'Hello', and wait.
   C Say, 'I think it's a mistake.'

2 A stranger says, 'Hello' and calls you by your first name. What do you do?
   A Try to read their conference name badge before replying.
   B Say, 'How are you? Are you still working for the same company?'
   C Say, 'You know me, but I don't know you. Sorry.'

3 You greet an acquaintance from another company. The acquaintance looks at you – and doesn't remember you. What do you do?
   A Shake hands, smile, and say your name and company.
   B Say, 'Do you remember me?'
   C Feel angry and walk away.

3 Don't I know you?

What do you say when you can't remember someone's name? Complete the spaces with *me*, *you*, or *each other*.

1 Don't I know .... ?

2 Don't we know .... ?

3 Do you remember .... ?

Forms of address

1 Forms of address

What do you call people when you meet them?
– your boss
   I call her by her surname, Mrs (Grant). / I call her by her first name, Susan. / I call her 'Ma'am'.

– shop assistants
   I don't call them anything.

– nurses
   I call them 'Nurse'.

What do you call these people?
– your best friend
– your doctor
– a waiter
– your co-workers
– a taxi driver
– your dentist
– a stranger on a train
– your English teacher
– an elderly man
– an elderly woman
– a male police officer
– a very famous rock star

2 What do they call you?

What does your boss call you?
She calls me by my first name.
She calls me by my surname.
She calls me by my job title.

What do these people call you?
– your doctor
– shop assistants
– younger relatives (e.g. nieces, nephews)
– co-workers
– waiters
– your teacher

3 Pronunciation

Say these words aloud. They are all in Unit one. The underlined sounds are the same.

were	sir	earn	prefer
title	sign	smile	mind
friend	weather	empty	remember
shake	great	say	aquaintance
bow	now	how	town
warm	formal	normal	form
student	new	you	few
greet	speak	meal	evening

4 First names

The chart shows the most popular names for children born in 1993.

England and Wales*

boys		girls	
1	Daniel	1	Rebecca
2	Matthew	2	Charlotte
3	James	3	Laura
4	Christopher	4	Amy
5	Thomas	5	Emma
6	Joshua	6	Jessica

United States

boys		girls	
1	Michael	1	Brittany
2	Christopher	2	Ashley
3	Matthew	3	Jessica
4	Joshua	4	Amanda
5	Andrew	5	Sarah
6	James	6	Megan

Australia

boys		girls	
1	Matthew	1	Jessica
2	James	2	Sarah
3	Thomas	3	Emily
4	Joshua	4	Rebecca
5	Benjamin	5	Emma
6	Daniel	6	Hannah

* The statistics are for England and Wales only. Scotland and Northern Ireland have different lists.

Answer these questions.
– Do you know the most popular names for your country? If not, try and guess. Make a list for boys and girls.
– Are they different from what they were thirty years ago?
– What are your favourite first names in your language?
– What are your favourite first names in English?

Starting a conversation

1 Adjectives

Complete this 'instant postcard' by completing the spaces and ticking the boxes.

Dear ....,

The flight was ❑ early ❑ on time ❑ delayed.
Our plane was ❑ full ❑ empty ❑ 30 years old.
The flight attendants were ❑ excellent
❑ impolite ❑ wearing parachutes.
Our hotel is ❑ big ❑ small ❑ old ❑ dirty.
Our room is ❑ excellent ❑ terrible ❑ next to the
disco ❑ above the kitchens.
The food is very ❑ good ❑ bad ❑ cold.
We're very ❑ pleased ❑ sorry ❑ lucky to be here.

Best wishes,

....

Instant Postcard

Ms K
Flat
Alba
St S
Bren
Ess

2 Make the sentences negative

Write sentences as in the example.

The plane was full.
The plane wasn't full.

1 I was there on business.
2 The plane was on time.
3 They were friends.
4 We were busy.
5 Her car was in the car park.
6 She was American.
7 You were late.

3 Boarding pass

Look at the boarding pass and write short answers.

1 What was the flight number?
2 What was the airline?
3 What was the date of the flight?
4 What was her seat number?
5 What was the departure time?
6 What was the city of departure?
7 What was the destination?

Asking questions

1 Word order

Rewrite these questions in the correct order.

journey? / like / was / What / your / train
What was your train journey like?

1 food? / think / you / French / of / What / do
2 staying / long / you / are / How / here?
3 like / country? / What / your / weather / was / the / in
4 here? / your / Is / visit / this / first
5 your / OK / hotel? / Is / at / everything
6 do? / do / you / What

2 Open conversation

Imagine you are at an airport in your country. You are waiting for an English visitor. Complete the conversation.

YOU: Hello. You must be ....

VISITOR: Yes, that's right.

YOU: My name's ....

....

VISITOR: Pleased to meet you, too. And thank you for coming to meet me.

YOU: ....

.... ?

VISITOR: Oh, OK. I don't really enjoy flying. I'm glad to be back on the ground!

YOU: .... ?

VISITOR: No, it isn't. I was here last year, but only for a few days.

YOU: .... ?

VISITOR: Seventeen days. I'm flying home on the 24th.

YOU: .... ?

VISITOR: It was raining when I left!

YOU: .... ?

VISITOR: I live in Dorchester. It's in the south of England. Do you know it?

YOU: .... ?

VISITOR: It's a small town in the country. No skyscrapers, or anything. It's a typical old country town. There are lots of good pubs!

YOU: .... Ah, this is my car. Let me take your suitcase.

Closing a conversation

In Unit one, the theme was opening and closing.

☛ See **formula** in the Student's Book **Glossary**.

1 **Which area of language is most useful in opening and closing a conversation?**
   – formulas
   – structures
   – vocabulary

2 **Which sentences below are formulas?**
1 Have a nice day!
2 There you go.
3 We were late yesterday.
4 The plane was empty.
5 How do you do.
6 Which one do you like?
7 I'd like to meet your brother.
8 Nice to see you again.

3 **Closing formulas**
Look in the Student's Book. Complete the spaces.

1 I .... to see you next time I come to London.
2 I look .... to seeing you again soon.
3 Take .... of yourself.
4 .... a good weekend.
5 Enjoy the .... of your stay.

After you've finished

Skills check

Here are three lists of some of the communication topics from Unit one of the Student's Book. How confident do you feel about doing these things? Write *A* – very confident, *B* – quite confident, or *C* – need more practice.

First list

..... Can you greet people in formal and informal situations?
..... Can you introduce a friend to an acquaintance?
..... Can you begin a conversation by asking questions?
..... Can you close a conversation?

Second list

..... Can you remember the intonation of 'Fine, thanks. And you?'
..... Can you greet your boss (headteacher) in English?
..... Can you thank a friend after a meal?
..... Can you hear the difference between '17' and '70'?

Third list

..... Can you remember the advice about shaking hands?
..... Can you remember how English people greet each other?
..... Can you remember what you did in the role-plays?
..... Can you use different forms of address?

Think about this. Which list do you prefer as a reminder of unit one? Look at the box below.

Visual learners usually prefer the first list.
Auditory learners usually prefer the second list.
Kinaesthetic learners usually prefer the third list.

Grammar check

You can test yourself. Choose the correct word.

1 It's great (see / to see / meet) you again!
2 How are you (do / to do / doing)?
3 Shake hands (strong / firm / firmly).
4 I'd like you (meet / to meet / meeting) Ms Azegami from Japan.
5 Where (you / do you / are you) live?
6 (May / Would / Am) I introduce Kevin Costner?
7 I ('m not / don't / doesn't) remember your name.
8 Laura (don't / doesn't / isn't) know Mr Costello.
9 Does she (like / to like / likes) French food?
10 Where (does / do / are) you come from?
11 I'm (go / going / will) to visit some customers.
12 Where are you (stay / to stay / staying)?
13 How (age / many years / old) are you?
14 How (are / were / was) your flight?
15 Good night. Nice to have (met / meeting / meet) you.
16 Where do (she / they / I) usually have lunch?
17 (Doesn't / Can't / Don't) ask him. He doesn't know.
18 *Be careful!* is an (infinitive / imperative / adjective).
19 *That was nice.* This sentence is (present / future / past).
20 I'm going to see him (yesterday / usually / tomorrow).

Here are the answers to 'How do you learn?' on page 11.

Mostly 'A's: You are probably a visual learner. i.e. You prefer learning through seeing.
Mostly 'B's: You are probably an auditory learner. i.e. You prefer learning through hearing.
Mostly 'C's: You are probably a kinaesthetic learner. i.e. You prefer learning through moving, doing, and touching.
Two of each: You are amazingly well-balanced. Are you sure you gave true answers?

UNIT TWO
Non-verbal communication

Thinking about learning

Positive attitudes

All of us sometimes feel positive about learning, and all of us sometimes feel negative. We learn more effectively when we're feeling positive. Look at the statements below.

I'm learning English because I have to.

I'd like to travel to English-speaking countries.

English will help my career.

I'm embarrassed about my accent in English.

People who make mistakes are stupid.

I can always make people understand me.

I feel tired during English lessons and can't concentrate.

If you're friendly and smile, English speakers don't worry about your mistakes.

There are lots of opportunities for me to hear English.

I feel pleased when I can understand English words on packets or in advertisements.

Some people are natural linguists.

It's more difficult to learn English when you are older.

I don't get high grades in English exams.

My personality is different when I'm speaking English.

1 Which of the statements are true for you?
2 Divide the statements into positive (+) and negative (−).
3 Assess yourself. Do you have mostly positive or negative attitudes?

Reasons for learning

Why are you learning English? There are some reasons below. Tick the appropriate boxes.

Reason for learning English	very important				not important
Because I have to	☐	☐	☐	☐	☐
Because I want to	☐	☐	☐	☐	☐
Because my parents / company want me to	☐	☐	☐	☐	☐
Because English is a world language	☐	☐	☐	☐	☐
So I can get a better job	☐	☐	☐	☐	☐
So I can travel to different countries	☐	☐	☐	☐	☐
So I can pass an examination	☐	☐	☐	☐	☐
Because I'm going to visit an English-speaking country	☐	☐	☐	☐	☐
Because I want to emigrate to an English-speaking country	☐	☐	☐	☐	☐
So I can speak to visitors to my country	☐	☐	☐	☐	☐
Because it's something to do – I meet people at classes	☐	☐	☐	☐	☐
So I can understand books, magazines, technical manuals, TV, films, or rock songs in English	☐	☐	☐	☐	☐
Because I want to practise the English I already know	☐	☐	☐	☐	☐
Another reason (write it in here)					

Are your reasons the same as other people in your class? Find out.

Gesture

1 Arm and hand

Complete the diagram by writing in the words below.

arm	elbow	fingernail	index finger
hand	little finger	middle finger	palm
wrist	shoulder	ring finger	thumb

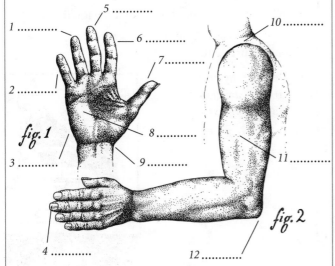

5 ....
1 ....
6 ....
10 ....
7 ....
2 ....
fig.1
8 ....
3 ....
9 ....
11 ....
fig.2
4 ....
12 ....

2 Matching

Look at the Student's Book. Match the words from the first column with words from the second column.

Be	away.
Keep	that!
Go	quiet!
Come	here.
Don't do	calm.

2 British or American English?

Look at these pairs of words. One in each pair is British, and the other is American. Underline the American words.

pants / trousers	waistcoat / vest
colour / color	jewelry / jewellery
purse / handbag	moustache / mustache
brooch / pin	undershirt / vest
grey / gray	undershorts / underpants
pyjamas / pajamas	robe / dressing gown
trainers / sneakers	tights / panty-hose

3 Find the differences

Look at both pictures.
Make sentences using these verbs.

touching, drinking, wearing, eating, holding, looking at

In picture 1, he's looking at her.
In picture 2, he's looking at his cup of tea.

Dress and appearance

1 Clothes

Put these words onto the chart. You can use a dictionary.

wig, skirt, tie, ear-ring(s), trainers (USA – sneakers), suit, trousers (USA – pants), overcoat (USA – topcoat), T-shirt, hat, cardigan, boots, shorts, shirt, scarf, jacket, helmet, leggings, dress, blouse, socks, sweatshirt, necklace, tracksuit, sweater, raincoat, shoes, nose-stud

on the head	around the neck	top half of the body	bottom half of the body	both halves of the body	on top of other clothes	on the feet

4 both

Make sentences which are true about both people.

They're both drinking something.

5 Making questions

He's writing something.
What's he writing?

Make questions in the same way.

1 She's going somewhere.
2 We're doing something.
3 They're watching something.
4 I'm looking at someone.
5 You're reading something.
6 He's thinking about someone.
7 It's flying somewhere.

Body language

1 look, feel, taste, smell, sound

Look at the words below, and make a sentence for each one using *look, feel, taste, smell,* or *sound.*

coffee	*It smells good.*
puppies	*They look cute (USA) / sweet (UK).*

rap music	chili peppers	a baby's hand
cold fries	chewing gum	a dentist's drill
snakes	doughnuts	kittens (baby cats)
ketchup	red lipstick	old trainers
cigars	peppermints	Chanel No. 5

Here are some adjectives to help you.

soft	cold	hot	horrible	disgusting
terrible	cute	sweet	awful	wonderful
good	warm	lovely	nice	

2 Complete the spaces

Put *look, feel, taste, smell,* or *sound* into the spaces. Use each of them once only. Read all the sentences before you begin!

1 Her perfume .... like summer flowers.

2 Put a shell to your ear. It .... like the sea.

3 Ergh! The water from the kitchen tap .... like water from a swimming pool!

4 That woman is very good-looking. She .... like Princess Diana.

5 This cardigan's very soft. It .... like 100% wool, but it isn't. It's acrylic.

3 What are they doing? How do they look?

Look at the example, and write sentences about pictures 2 to 4.

1 *He's leaning back.
His eyes are closed.
He looks relaxed.*

2 ....
   ....
   ....

3 ....
   ....
   ....

4 ....
   ....
   ....

Facial expression

1 worried / worrying

*The news on TV was very **worrying**. I was very
worried.*
*The movie was pretty **boring**. We were **bored**.*

Complete the spaces either the *-ing* adjective
(e.g. *worrying*) or the *-ed* adjective (e.g. *worried*).

1 You should read this book. It's very
  (interesting / interested).
2 I always feel very (relaxing / relaxed) after
  a hot bath.
3 She was very (depressing / depressed) after
  she failed her exams.
4 The journey was very long and (tiring /
  tired).
5 His behaviour is very (embarrassing /
  embarrassed) when he's drunk.
6 She was (surprising / surprised) when she
  won £10,000 in the lottery.
7 Their parents were very (annoying /
  annoyed) with them.

2 being boring / being bored

In exercise 1, you used the *-ing* adjective for
things and the *-ed* adjective for people. But
you can use both forms with a different
meaning for people.

boring / bored
*He's a very **boring** speaker. I'm very **bored**
when I listen to him.*

Complete the spaces.

1 depressing / depressed
  He's always miserable. He's a very ....
  person. I feel .... when I'm with him.
2 annoying / annoyed
  I feel really .... when my boss is rude
  to me. Actually, I think she's a very ....
  person.
3 interesting / interested
  John's a very .... man. He knows some
  wonderful stories, and people are always
  .... when he's talking.

Making the right noises

1 Two-word verbs with *back*

There are many two-word verbs in English.
Here are some examples with *back*.

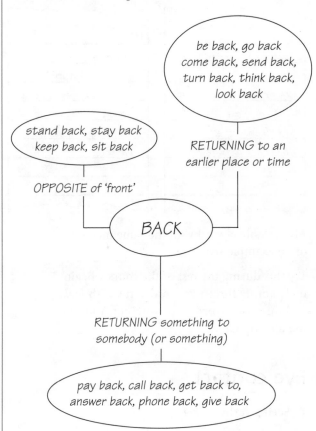

Write the verbs in the spaces (there may be
more than one correct answer).

1 Can you lend me $10? I'll .... you back
  next week.
2 I'm in a meeting at the moment. Can you
  .... me back in half an hour?
3 That dog looks dangerous. .... back.
4 I often .... back to when I was a child.
5 Sorry, I'm just going out for lunch. I'll
  .... back at two o'clock.
6 The climbers had to .... back because
  of heavy snow.
7 You're too close to the picture. ....
  back and you'll see it better.

3 Learning two-word verbs

You can note two- and three-word verbs in two ways. You can list them under the verb (*pay*) or under the preposition or particle (*back*).

pay
pay back = repay
pay into – e.g. pay
money into an account
pay for – e.g. She paid
for the tickets.
pay back for = revenge

back
pay back = repay
go back = return
send back – e.g. I don't
want this catalogue.
I'm going to send it
back.

Always note a word with the same meaning or an example sentence.

Try this during the rest of the course. Begin now, noting three two-word verbs with *look*, and three two-word verbs with *out*. You can use a dictionary.

Eye contact

1 Seeing verbs

Remember:
- you usually *watch* something that is moving
- you usually *look at* something that is still
- you hardly ever use *see* in continuous tenses.

Complete the spaces with the correct form of *see*, *look*, or *watch*.

1 'Hello? Susan? Can you come and .... me next week?'

2 100,000 people are in the stadium. They're .... the football match.

3 'Open your mouth,' said the dentist. 'I want to .... at your tooth.'

4 'I love .... in shop windows.'

5 'What's that over there? Can you .... it?'

6 She normally .... TV after dinner.

7 I hate .... at myself in the mirror.

2 Body expressions

Find the meaning of the body expressions in *italic* text. Is the correct meaning A, B, or C?

STORE DETECTIVE: 'Hmm. He's a shifty looking person. I'm going to *keep an eye on him*.'

A have a lot of eye contact with him
B watch him carefully all the time
C send a private detective to follow him

STUDENT: 'Sorry, the answer's *on the tip of my tongue*, just give me a minute … no, I can't remember it. Wait …'

A The answer is extremely difficult.
B I don't know the answer.
C I know the correct answer, but I can't actually remember it at the moment.

TEACHER: 'There are fifteen English words in this unit. I want you to *learn them by heart* this evening.'

A love learning them
B memorize them
C translate them

MAN WITH SEVERAL SHOPPING BAGS: 'Don't just stand there, Jennifer! *Give me a hand*.'

A shake hands with me
B show your appreciation by clapping your hands
C help me

STUDENT: 'My last class finishes at five, but my bus leaves at 4.55. The next one's at 5.55. It's a real *pain in the neck*.'

A It's very annoying.
B My neck hurts.
C Waiting a long time gives me a headache.

1ST PERSON: 'I don't know what to do about this question.'
2ND PERSON: 'Neither do I. But if we *put our heads together*, we'll find the answer.'

A sit next to each other
B co-operate and work together
C do a role-play

Position

1 Prepositions

Label the diagrams with these words.

behind	in front of	between	beside

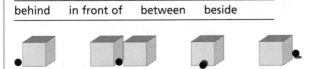

2 A business meeting

There is a business meeting at Telstar Micro-systems. Where are people sitting? Read all the notes below. Then label the chairs on the diagram with the people's initials.

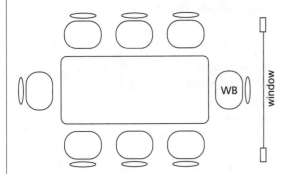

Will Bates (WB), the Managing Director of Telstar, has his back to the window.

Rachel Sculley from Grapefruit Computers is sitting opposite him. She's trying to buy Telstar Micro-systems.

Bill Forbes, Will's personal assistant, is sitting on the left of his boss. He's taking notes.

Tania Olivetti, the Sales Director of Telstar, is sitting opposite Bill Forbes.

Belinda Myers is Rachel's assistant. She's sitting on the same side of the table as Tania Olivetti.

James Hepworth-Smythe is the company accountant at Telstar. He's sitting between two women.

Gurnam Singh is the Finance Director of Grapefruit. Rachel thinks of him as her right-hand man … and that's where he's sitting.

Lian Chang is the company lawyer at Telstar. She's sitting in the middle of one side of the table.

Proximity

1 *too / very*

Complete the spaces with *very* or *too*.

1 The tickets are £5 for adults, and £3 for children under fourteen. He's fifteen so he's .... old for a child ticket.

2 He's .... young, but he can play the guitar well.

3 The exercise was .... difficult, but I answered everything correctly.

4 The plane left at 11.00. I arrived at five past. I was .... late.

5 We arrived at their house at 8.20. We apologized because we were .... late.

6 I can't understand anything at all. It's much .... difficult for me.

7 The film has an '18' certificate. She's sixteen, so she's .... young to see it.

8 Thank you for the present! It's .... nice.

2 Comparisons

Note how the spelling changes.

adjectives: *long, big, close, friendly*
comparatives: *longer, bigger, closer, friendlier*

Complete this table.

adjective	comparative
far	....
strong	....
near	....
hard	....
cold	....
warm	....
sad	....
large	....
sexy	....
silly	....
shifty	....

Touching

This Workbook section introduces a new topic, queueing, with similar language to touching. Do this section quickly. In British English the standard expression is *queueing*. In the United States it's *standing in line*, but both expressions are understood in both countries.

1 How often?

Complete the spaces in these sentences with one of these words: *always, never, often, sometimes, hardly ever.*

1 People in Britain .... queue.

2 People in the USA .... stand in line.

3 People in my country .... queue.

2 Where do you queue?

Where do people in your country stand in line? Tick the boxes.

..... bus-stops
..... ticket offices
..... banks
..... post offices
..... airport check-in counters
..... supermarket check-outs
..... fast food restaurants
..... self-service cafeterias
..... bars
..... shops
..... public toilets

Now you've finished exercise 2, do you want to change your answer in exercise 1? People in nearly all cultures queue at airports, supermarkets, and fast food restaurants.

3 How do you feel?

How do you feel when you're standing in line?

– Relaxed. I don't mind standing in line. I can talk to my neighbours.
– Nervous. I'm afraid someone will push in, or that my queue will be slower than the next one.
– Annoyed. I hate wasting time. I complain about the time, the queue, and the servers.
– Depressed. The queues are very long and slow.

4 Do you agree?

Grade these statements from *5* (agree strongly) to *1* (disagree strongly).

..... Queues are fairer. Everyone gets the same chance. They're better for old people, pregnant women, people with children, etc.
..... Queues are bureaucratic, and against individual freedom.
..... Queues are a good way of meeting people and having friendly conversations.

Status symbols

1 Comparison

The five smallest countries in the world		
country	location	area (square kilometres)
1 Vatican City	Italy	0.4
2 Monaco	France	1.9
3 Nauru	Pacific Ocean	21
4 Tuvalu	Pacific Ocean	26
5 San Marino	Italy	61

The five cities in the USA with the greatest populations (1990)	
city	population
1 New York	7,322,564
2 Los Angeles	3,485,398
3 Chicago	2,783,726
4 Houston	1,630,553
5 Philadelphia	1,585,577

The least popular jobs around the house (% is the percentage of people who said this was the worst job)
1 Washing the dishes 61%
2 Cleaning the bathroom 18%
3 Ironing clothes 9%
4 Making the beds 7%
5 Cooking 3%
Other answers 2%

The most popular ice-cream flavours in Britain (% is the percentage of people who prefer the flavour)
1 Vanilla 39%
2 Chocolate 18%
3 Strawberry 17%
4 Lemon sorbet 6%
5 Coffee 4%
Other flavours 16%

How many sentences can you make?

Which is smaller, Tuvalu or San Marino?
San Marino is smaller than Tuvalu.
Which is the smallest?
Vatican City is the smallest.

Use these comparisons.

smaller / the smallest
larger area / the largest area
bigger / the biggest
greater population / the greatest population
more popular / the most popular
less popular / the least popular

2 Your country

Look at this information.

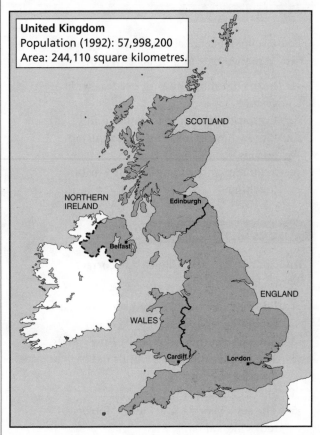

United Kingdom
Population (1992): 57,998,200
Area: 244,110 square kilometres.

SCOTLAND
NORTHERN IRELAND
Edinburgh
Belfast
ENGLAND
WALES
Cardiff
London

First complete the spaces in these questions, then write full answers to them.

1 Is your country bigger or .... than the UK?

2 Does it have a .... population than the UK?

3 Is the capital city of your country the .... city in the country?

4 What ice-cream flavour do you like .... ?

5 Which job around the house do you like .... ?

3 Find the words

1 Write down five things which are bigger than a bus.

2 Write down five things which are smaller than a CD.

27

After you've finished

These statements are about topics from unit two. Are they true (✔) or false (✘) for you?

..... I can communicate a lot of ideas with gesture.
..... I can use intonation to sound polite.
..... I know how to look interested during lessons.
..... I can remember five different words for touching.

Grammar check

You can test yourself. Choose the correct word.

1 I'd like (they / their / them) to work late tonight.
2 Can you get that book for (I / me / my)?
3 The teacher wants (we / our / us) to describe the picture.
4 She seems (angrily / angry).
5 The sky's very dark. It (look / looks / to look) like rain.
6 He's (write / writes / writing) a letter.
7 What (are / do / can) you doing?
8 She isn't (listening / to listen / listen) to the lesson.
9 I want (to buy / buy / buying) a new pair of trainers.
10 I often (goes / going / go) to the cinema.
11 The sun (usually / never / always) goes down in the west.
12 I'm (normally / usually / hardly) ever late for work.
13 She was (very / too / much) tired to go out.
14 Her office is (large / larger / largest) than my office.
15 I'd like a (better / best / well) job.
16 People in the city stand (closely / closest / closer) than people in the country.
17 This car is (less / most / least) comfortable than that one.
18 How (ever / often / usually) do you go to the theatre?
19 (Could / Do / May) you bring me the bill?
20 (Aren't / Doesn't / Don't) be silly!

Thinking about learning

Assessing your own abilities

1 Application form

This is a section from an application form.
Complete it with your details.

> #### Section 4: Language ability in English
>
> 1 Which foreign languages do you speak?
>
> _____
>
> 2 How long have you been studying English?
>
> _____
>
> 3 Have you passed any examinations in English?
>   Which one(s)?
>
> _____
>
> 4 Assess your standard in English:
>   ❏ Beginner ❏ Elementary / False beginner
>   ❏ Intermediate ❏ Fluent / Advanced
>
> 5 Have you visited any English-speaking countries?
>   Which one(s)?
>
> _____

2 Skills in English

Assess your ability in the skills below. Use
these expressions.

I'm very good at …
I'm good at …
I'm average at …
I'm not very good at …
I'm hopeless at …

- speaking in English
- listening (understanding people)
- reading
- writing
- spelling
- pronunciation
- grammar
- learning vocabulary

Then complete these sentences.

I have most difficulty with …
I have least difficulty with …
I need more work on …

3 Ways of learning

Tick the activities that you do. Then make
sentences about yourself with:

I enjoy …
I don't mind …
I don't like …

..... doing grammar exercises
..... studying grammar
..... learning vocabulary
..... practising pronunciation
..... doing tests
..... dictation
..... translation
..... watching videos
..... listening to spoken English recordings
..... listening to songs
..... listening to the teacher
..... doing reading comprehension exercises
..... reading for pleasure
..... writing
..... working with computers
..... using the Internet
..... conversation practice with a partner
..... having discussions
..... doing role-play and drama activities
..... other activities
....

Write answers to these questions.
- Which of the activities do you like doing in
  class?
- Which of the activities do you prefer doing
  at home?
- Which is the most useful activity for you?
- Which is the least useful activity for you?
- Which is your favourite activity?

Personal information

Home Sweet Home

Home Sweet Home is a new TV soap opera about a typical English family, the Smiths. Read the information about the programme. Imagine a similar programme about a typical family in your country. Write information about the characters in your programme.

COMING TO YOUR SCREENS SOON!

CHANNEL 5's NEW FAMILY SOAP,
Home Sweet Home

YOU'LL LOVE THE CHARACTERS!

Bob Smith
Bob Smith is 43 and lives in Manchester. He's a sales representative for Finlay's Frozen Food. Bob drives a new Rover car (and he's very proud of it!). He belongs to a golf club, and plays golf every weekend.

Lisa Smith
Lisa Smith is 41. She works in a bank. She drives a second-hand red Mini. Lisa is interested in antiques. She has an antique stall in the local market on Saturdays. Lisa goes to an aerobics class twice a week.

Kylie Smith
Kylie is 18. She's studying pyschology at the local college. Kylie has a part-time job on Saturdays. She works in a shoe shop. Kylie is saving up to buy a car. She likes dance music and goes dancing three times a week.

Craig Smith
Craig is 15 and he's still at school. Craig plays football for his school on Saturday mornings, and spends Saturday afternoons watching Manchester United. He spends Saturday evenings watching football on TV.

Origins

Bharati Mukherjee, American novelist and university professor, was born in Calcutta, India and educated by Irish nuns. She moved to the USA in 1961 when she was 18. She received a Ph.D. from the University of Iowa. Her novels  include *Jasmine* and *The Holder of The World*.

William Shatner, actor, film director, and writer, was born in Montreal, Canada in 1931. He was educated at McGill University in Montreal, and graduated from McGill in 1952. He became famous as Captain Kirk in the *Star Trek* TV series from 1966. He later starred in the movies *Star Trek I–VI* and *Star Trek Generations*.

Margot Fonteyn, ballet dancer, was born in Reigate, England on May 18, 1919. She was brought up in Shanghai, China. She first appeared with the Sadler's Wells Ballet in London in 1934. She married Roberto Arias, a Panamanian politician, in 1955. Her famous dancing partnership with the Russian dancer Rudolf Nureyev began in 1962. She died in Panama City in 1991.

Freddie Mercury, singer with rock group Queen, was born in Zanzibar (now in Tanzania) in 1946. His real name was Frederick Bulsara. He went to school in India. His family moved to England in 1959. He joined Queen in 1971. Their most famous record was *Bohemian Rhapsody*. Mercury died in London in 1991.

1 Bharati Mukherjee

Read the text and complete the details on this card.

Family name	....
First name	....
Title (Mr / Mrs / Miss / Ms / Dr, etc.)	....
Place of birth	....
Nationality	....
Education	....
	....
Novels	....
	....

2 William Shatner

Read the text, then write a similar personal details card for William Shatner.

3 Margot Fonteyn

Write answers to the questions.

1 Where was she born?
2 When was she born?
3 Where was she brought up?
4 When did she marry Roberto Arias?
5 When did she begin dancing with Nureyev?
6 When did she die?
7 Where did she die?

4 Freddie Mercury

Write questions about Freddie Mercury, then answer them.

Your life and skills

1 Word order

Rewrite these questions in the correct order.

work? / you / do / Where
Where do you work?

1 you / have? / do / What / qualifications
2 any / you / Do / hobbies? / have
3 time? / you / What / like / free / doing / do / your / in
4 can / Which / speak? / languages / you
5 instrument? / you / a / Can / musical / play
6 things? / you / at / good / selling / Are
7 thinking / ideas? / of / Are / at / good / you / new

2 Your life

Answer these questions with complete sentences.

1 Where were you born?
2 Where were your parents born?
3 Where did you first go to school?
4 How many children were there in the class?
5 Who did you sit next to then?
6 What was your first teacher's name?
7 When did you begin English lessons?

3 Abilities

Which of these things can you do? Which of them can't you do? Make sentences with *and, but,* or *or.*

I can speak English, **but** *I can't speak German.*
I can speak English **and** *German.*
I can't speak English **or** *German.*

1 speak French /speak Spanish
2 drive a car / drive a truck
3 play the piano / play the guitar
4 use a computer / program a computer
5 understand written English / understand spoken English
6 ride a bicycle / ride a horse

Checking information

1 School subjects

Look at this list of school subjects. Which ones do / did you study? Underline them. Add any other subjects to the list.

..... mathematics	..... sociology
..... physics	..... media studies
..... chemistry	..... politics / civics
..... biology	..... economics
..... technology	..... business studies
..... computer studies	..... typing
..... your language	..... art
..... English	..... music
..... another language	..... physical education
..... history	..... textile technology
..... geography	..... domestic science
..... religious studies	..... car mechanics

Which ones do you think school students should study? Tick them. (✔)

2 Question tags

Add question tags to these sentences.

1 You studied biology at school, ... ?

2 You didn't study music, ... ?

3 You can't operate a computer, ... ?

4 You can type, ... ?

5 You haven't failed an English exam, ... ?

6 You've taken several exams, ... ?

7 You don't play the piano, ... ?

8 You were good at art, ... ?

3 Words ending in -ist

SEISMOLOGISTS PREDICT 7.2 EARTHQUAKE!

ECONOMIST DISAGREES WITH SYSTEMS ANALYSTS

FERGIE VISITS NEW-AGE THERAPIST

GENETICIST DISCOVERS DINOSAUR D.N.A.

TERRORISTS ATTACK TOURISTS' BUS

PSYCHIATRIST CRITICIZES HYPNOTISTS

subject / activity: *science*   instrument: *guitar*
person: *scientist*   person: *guitarist*

Complete the spaces in this table.

subject / activity	person
art	....
pharmacy	....
....	typist
biochemistry	....
....	physicist
biology	....
....	psychologist

instrument	person
violin	....
piano	....
....	vocalist
....	saxophonist
organ	....
clarinet	....
percussion	....

4 More words ending in -ist

Complete the spaces in these sentences.

1 Someone who writes for journals (i.e. newspapers and magazines) is a ....

2 Someone who deals with dental problems is a ....

3 Someone who receives visitors in a hotel or office is a ....

4 Someone who believes in socialism is a ....

Saying the wrong thing

1 Matching

Match the sentences (1–7) with the replies (A–G).

1 Have you ever been to Florida?
2 Would you like a coffee?
3 Have you seen the new Disney cartoon?
4 I've just bought an Everest Computer.
5 How long have you worked here?
6 Have you had a vacation this year?
7 Hi! I haven't seen you for ages!

A No, thanks. I've already had one.
B I've never heard of them. Is it any good?
C Not long. About two months.
D I'm sorry. I've forgotten your name.
E Yes, I've been there twice.
F Not yet. I'm going to see it next week.
G No, we've been too busy.

2 *already, ever, never, yet*

Complete the spaces in these sentences.

1 We haven't finished unit three ....

2 Have you .... been to Canada?

3 She's only fourteen, and she's .... studied five languages.

4 No, he's .... been to France.

5 Has your company .... exported goods to Britain?

6 I've .... applied for three jobs, but no one has replied.

7 We haven't had a coffee break ....

8 I've heard of him, but I've .... met him.

3 Past participles

Look back at exercises 1 and 2. Find the past participles of these verbs.

finish	export	have	hear	see
apply	study	reply	forget	meet

4 Vocabulary: jobs and qualities

What qualities do people need for these jobs? Make one sentence about each job.

A pilot needs to be reliable.
A pilot needs to have good eyesight.

a pilot	intelligent
a sales representative	co-operative
a waiter	good eyesight
a nurse	ambitious
a radio DJ	sympathetic
a receptionist	a nice voice
a hairdresser	friendly
a primary teacher	cheerful
a police officer	sincere
	confident
	punctual
	honest
	loyal
	reliable
	polite
	healthy
	patient
	strong
	a sense of humour
	pleasant appearance
	interested in people

Receiving information

1 Making calls and receiving calls

Look at the sentences. Think about them carefully. Which ones are said by:
– a person making a call? (Write *A*)
– a person receiving a call? (Write *B*)

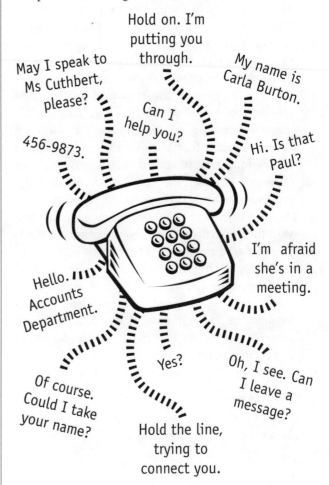

May I speak to Ms Cuthbert, please?

Hold on. I'm putting you through.

My name is Carla Burton.

Can I help you?

456-9873.

Hi. Is that Paul?

Hello. Accounts Department.

I'm afraid she's in a meeting.

Of course. Could I take your name?

Yes?

Hold the line, trying to connect you.

Oh, I see. Can I leave a message?

2 Reading – Telephone virus?

> **bear with sb/sth** to show patience, etc towards sb/sth: *We must bear with her* (ie treat her with sympathy) *during this difficult period.* • *If you will bear with me* (ie be patient and listen to me) *a little longer, I'll answer your question.*

From the *Oxford Advanced Learner's Dictionary*

Read the text on the next page.

1 Underline the expressions you can use when you ask someone to wait on the phone.

2 Which four adjectives are used to describe the expression *Bear with me*?

Fashions, ideas, and speech habits spread like viruses in modern society. In the mid 1980s Americans usually said 'There you go' while the British said 'Here you are.' By the late 1980s, 'There you go' was as popular in Britain as 'Here you are'. By the mid 1990s, it was more popular.

Telephone operators have always used formulas. The traditional ones in Britain were 'Hold the line' or 'Please hold' (for any delay) and 'Trying to connect you' (for a delay in connecting you to the right person). By the early 1990s there were many mail order companies which were taking orders on the phone. At some point, an operator somewhere started saying 'Bear with me' while they were finding information from a computer screen. It was a formal and rather old-fashioned expression, but it spread like a virus. Soon operators all over the country were using the expression. Why? Perhaps it was a particularly useful expression. The operators were dealing with the problems themselves, not connecting you to another department. They weren't 'trying to connect you' and you weren't 'holding the line' until someone else answered. They were simply asking you to wait and to be patient. 'Just a moment' or 'Just a minute' suggested a very short wait. 'Bear with me' was an old expression which fitted the situation exactly.

3 Matching

Look at the text. Then match the verbs in the first column with the words in the second column.

deal	the phone
trying	like a virus
answer	to connect you
fit	an order by phone
spread	with a problem
take	the situation

4 Find the different sound

All these words are from unit three. Put a ring around the word in each line which has a different underlined vowel sound.

h<u>o</u>tel	ph<u>o</u>ne	z<u>e</u>ro	g<u>o</u>lf
<u>e</u>cho	rep<u>ea</u>t	sp<u>e</u>ll	j<u>e</u>t
m<u>a</u>rital	h<u>a</u>lf	g<u>a</u>rbage	f<u>a</u>ther
st<u>a</u>tus	<u>a</u>ttend	r<u>a</u>ce	cr<u>ea</u>te
fl<u>u</u>ent	b<u>i</u>rth	s<u>u</u>rfing	<u>u</u>niversity
v<u>oi</u>ce	l<u>oy</u>al	empl<u>oy</u>er	bl<u>o</u>nde

h<u>ai</u>r	sinc<u>e</u>re	cl<u>ea</u>r	y<u>ea</u>r
<u>o</u>rganize	c<u>o</u>llege	d<u>au</u>ghter	sh<u>o</u>rt

Question types

1 Talking about an object

Here are some questions you can ask about almost any object. <u>Underline</u> the *Yes / No* questions.

External appearance
What is it?
What does it look like?
What colour is it?
What does it feel / smell / sound like?

Size / weight
How long is it?
How wide is it?
How big is it?
How much does it weigh?

Construction
What's it made of?
Is it made of natural or synthetic materials?
Who made it?
Was it made by hand?
Was it made by machine?

Function
What's it for?
What do we do with it?

Age
Is it new / modern / old?
How old is it?
When was it made?

Origin
Where does it come from?
Where's it from?
Who does it belong to?
Whose is it?
Where was it made?
Where did the materials come from?

Value
Is it valuable?
How much does / did it cost?
What is it worth?

Design
Is it well designed?
Is it decorated or plain?
How can you make it better?

Opinion
Do you like it?
Would you like one of these?
Is this example a good (one) or a bad (one)?
Is it beautiful / ugly / useful?

2 Choose a picture

Write as many questions as you can about it. You can use the questions in exercise 1 as a guide, or you can add your own questions. Then answer your questions. Only write questions that you can answer!

3 Word order

Put the words in the correct order to make questions from a job interview.

1 journey? / you / Did / good / a / have
2 long / company? / your / How / you / for / have / worked / present
3 you / speak? / many / languages / do / How
4 operate / you / computer? / Can / a / Macintosh
5 processing? / word / Have / studied / you
6 college? / you / did / When / leave
7 us / you / Would / to / any / like / questions? / ask

An interview

1 Someone's CV

CURRICULUM VITAE

Name:	Anthony David CRAWFORD
Date of birth:	19 February 1971
Present address:	Flat 4, Bleak House, 61 Corporation Street, Poole, Dorset BH13 3NG
Telephone:	01202-176334
Education:	1991 – 94 University of Blandford, B.Sc. in Biochemistry 1987 – 89 Branksome College, Poole 1982 – 87 St. Basil's School, Swanage
Work experience:	1996 – present Fastgro Fertilisers plc, Poole. Research assistant. 1994 – 96 Sunshine Detergents plc, Swindon. Trainee manager. 1993 (summer vacation) Teaching volleyball at Camp Granada, New Jersey, USA (children's summer camp).
Languages:	GCSE level: French, Latin
Other skills:	Voluntary work: Save the Whales campaign, 1992 – present (area secretary).
Sports:	captain of volleyball team at university.

References available on request.

Put the two parts of the questions together. Write eight questions. Then imagine that you are Anthony Crawford, and answer them.

first part
How long have you ...
When did you ...

second part
..... lived at your present address?
..... work for Sunshine Detergents?
..... leave school?
..... been at Fastgro?
..... take your GCSE in French?
..... go to Blandford University?
..... worked for Save the Whales?
..... had a B.Sc. degree?

2 Now or then?

Which questions refer to things that:
– were about the past and about the present?
– were about the past only?

3 Asking the questions

Interviewers don't ask all the questions. The interviewee should ask questions too. Which of these questions might you ask during an interview? Put a tick.(✓)

..... Do you mind if I smoke?
..... Can you tell me more about the job?
..... Could I have a glass of water?
..... What's the time? I have to catch a train.
..... Who's paying my travelling expenses?
..... How many weeks holiday are there?
..... Can I use the company phones for personal calls?
..... What's the starting salary?
..... Can I call you (Peter)?
..... Does the job include a company car?
..... Have I got the job?
..... When will I hear from you?
..... What did I do wrong?

4 Job adverts

Complete the spaces in this job advert. There is more than one possible answer.

BILINGUAL SECRETARY WANTED

FOR

CD-ROM DESIGN COMPANY

Needs to speak and .... English and ....
A third foreign .... is an advantage.
Excellent .... and working conditions.
Good .... for promotion.
.... with CV to:

Sea Dee Innovations, Pippin Business Park,
Newton Street, Appleton, AP3 4PC.

Interview assessment

Body language

In the wonderfully sophisticated age in which we live, more and more people are becoming aware of the science of body language. It now matters how we sit, what we do with our legs and arms and hands, and even how we walk into an interview. Crossed arms indicate a defensive attitude. Hands in trouser pockets is still considered impolite in the case of men, and one hand nonchalantly thrust into her jacket pocket by a woman is considered by some to indicate arrogance. Legs may be crossed, but not ostentatiously so, and not if such action reveals a stretch of flesh above the sock top in the case of men, or too much stockinged leg in the case of women.

From *Debrett's Guide to Business Etiquette* by Nicholas Yapp (Headline, 1994)

1 Vocabulary

Find words or phrases in the text which mean:

1 the modern world
2 it's important how we sit
3 thought by people to be rude
4 thought by some people to show you are arrogant
5 if you're a man
6 if you're a woman
7 you can cross your legs, but only if you do this carefully
8 several centimetres of naked leg
9 a woman's leg wearing stockings or tights.

2 *Don't ...*

The author is giving advice in the text.
Change his advice to a list of instructions.

Don't cross your arms.

3 Compound words

Match the words from the first column with words form the second column. All of the words are from unit three.

reception	control
eye	processing
rock	instrument
word	service
presidential	star
air traffic	contact
expiry	clerk
military	class
evening	date
musical	election

After you've finished

Skills check

How confident do you feel about doing these things in English?
Write A – very confident, B – fairly confident, C – not very confident.

..... talking about yourself
..... talking about your education
..... writing a CV
..... making a good impression in an interview

How do you feel about these things?
Write A – I can do this well, B – I can do this, but I have to think carefully, C – I need more practice.

..... taking a phone message in English
..... using the present perfect in conversation
..... asking questions to get information

Grammar check

You can test yourself. Choose the correct word.

1 Paul McCartney and John Lennon (were / was / are) born in Liverpool.
2 Her parents (got / get / are) married in Scotland.
3 When did you (leave / to leave / left) school?
4 Which schools (have / are / did) you attend?
5 He (didn't / wasn't / don't) go to university.
6 Are you good at working (with / by / at) yourself?
7 She's got a diploma in computer studies, (has / hasn't / isn't) she?
8 You didn't learn to type, (did you / isn't it / didn't you)?
9 Have you ever (go / been / went) to England?
10 How many jobs (has / did / have) he had?
11 I've (ever / always / never) been to New Zealand.
12 What do you do (by / for / during) your free time?
13 She spoke quietly but (confidently / confident / confiding).
14 How (often / long / much time) have you had your present job?
15 John F. Kennedy (has died / died / dying) in 1963.
16 Kennedy's ancestors were from (an Irishman / Ireland / Irish).
17 Can you (spell / spelling / to spell) your last name, please?
18 *I've been there* is (past / present / present perfect).
19 *Walk* is (regular / irregular / a verb) in the past tense.
20 *Done* is the (past simple / past participle / present perfect) of *do*.

UNIT FOUR
Social interaction

Thinking about learning

Types of intelligence

There are many different types of intelligence. Exams measure some types of intelligence, especially linguistic, logical, and factual intelligence. But exams can't measure everything. We all have a combination of several different kinds of intelligence. Look at the chart.

Type of intelligence	Abilities
linguistic	talking, reading, writing, learning languages
logical	maths, logical thinking, computing, organizing
factual	remembering facts
spatial (about space) /ˈspeɪʃl/	drawing, reading signs and pictures, parking a car, being aware of size and distance, thinking in pictures
physical	moving hands, moving body, playing sports, dancing
practical	taking things apart and putting them back together, assembling things, cooking
musical	singing, playing music, appreciating music, writing music
social	interested in people, co-operating, sympathizing, persuading, being friendly, caring for people
emotional	flexible, being optimistic, having self control, understanding your feelings, being confident
intuitive /ˌɪntjuːɪtɪv/	guessing, predicting, using instinct

Draw a bar graph to show your kinds of intelligence. Draw bars of different lengths on the chart below. For example, if you're very good at logical work you might give yourself 8 out of 10. If you're not very good at musical things you might give yourself 2 out of 10. If you're hopeless at intuitive things, don't draw a bar at all. Compare your chart with another student.

	1	2	3	4	5	6	7	8	9	10
linguistic										
logical										
factual										
spatial										
physical										
practical										
musical										
social										
emotional										
intuitive										

Put the words below onto the chart. You can put a word into more than one section if you like.

translator   mechanic   teacher   athlete
architect   salesperson   astrologer   parent
dancer   designer   accountant   writer
librarian   chef   doctor   singer
composer   scientist   taxi driver   sculptor
receptionist   lawyer   manager   footballer

Type of intelligence	Suitable jobs or social roles
linguistic	
logical	
factual	
spatial	
physical	
practical	
musical	
social	
emotional	
intuitive	

What would you say?

1 Verbs and nouns

Complete the spaces in this table. You can use a dictionary.

verb	noun
to refuse	a refusal
to	an offer
to suggest	a ....
to	permission
to apologize	an ....

2 Categories

Put the sentences in the correct boxes in the table.

1   Let's go and have lunch.
2   No, I won't do it.
3   May I leave early tonight?
4   I'm terribly sorry.
5   I'll do it for you.
6   Can I help you?
7   Can I borrow your pen?
8   Sorry, it's my fault.
9   Shall we stop for a moment?
10   Thank you, but no.

refusing
apologizing
making a suggestion
offering help
asking for permission

3 Nouns ending in -ion

Make nouns from these verbs. Either the verb or the noun has appeared in units one to four of the Student's Book.

suggest   *suggestion*

1   converse   ....
2   discuss   ....
3   introduce   ....
4   interact   ....
5   communicate   ....
6   demonstrate   ....
7   impress   ....
8   react   ....
9   express   ....
10   inform   ....
11   educate   ....
12   elect   ....
13   promote   ....
14   instruct   ....

Here are some more difficult examples. Either the verb or the noun has appeared in units one to four of the Student's Book. Note them with the other nouns from this exercise.

receive	reception
describe	description
observe	observation
present	presentation
imagine	imagination
interrogate	interrogation
graduate	graduation
qualify	qualification
pronounce	pronunciation

A cool reception

1 *Would you mind …?*

Would you mind doing this? is often a way of making a command or order into a polite request. Make the commands into polite requests.

Sign in.
Would you mind signing in?

Don't smoke.
Would you mind not smoking?

1 Wait outside the office.
2 Don't park here.
3 Don't leave your bags there.
4 Answer the phone.
5 Make us some coffee.
6 Move to another seat.
7 Don't talk in the library.

2 Object pronouns

Complete the spaces with object pronouns:
me, him, her, it, you, us, or *them.*

1 I'll call Mr Brown and tell .... you've arrived.
2 Good morning, madam. Can I help .... ?
3 Mrs Green is on the phone. Can you talk to .... ?
4 Sorry, I've put my keys somewhere, but I can't find ....
5 I can't speak now. Can you call .... later?
6 We can't find anywhere to park. Can you help .... ?
7 I can't find the exit. Which way is .... ?

3 Opposites

These words have all appeared in units one to four of the Student's Book. What are the opposites? Put them in the correct columns. You can use a dictionary.

happy	reliable	direct	sympathetic
polite	honest	sincere	popular
patient	attractive	loyal	agreeable
enthusiastic	ambitious	personal	formal
embarrassed	co-operative	comfortable	helpful

un-	in-	im-	dis-
unhappy			

Indirect questions

The grammar of indirect questions isn't difficult, but everyone needs a lot of practice. Write your answers to exercises 1 to 4, then return to the exercises next week and the week after and try doing them again quickly in your head.

☞ There will be more work on indirect questions in the **Language Focus** section of unit five in the Student's Book.

1 *to be* and *wh-* questions

Make indirect questions.

Whose is it?
Can you tell me whose it is?

What is that?
Can you tell me what that is?

1 What is this?
2 Whose are these?
3 Who is that?
4 Where are they?
5 When is it?
6 How much is there?
7 How many are there?
8 What time is it?
9 What are those?

2 *to be* and *wh*-questions

Make indirect questions.

What is your name?
Could you tell me what your name is?

Where are you from?
Could you tell me where you are from?

1 What is your address?
2 Where were you born?
3 What is your telephone number?
4 What time is your appointment?
5 Who are you meeting?
6 When are you going to leave?
7 Which one was he married to?

3 *do / does / did* and *wh-* questions

Make indirect questions.

When does the bank open?
Do you know when the bank opens?

Where did she go?
Do you know where she went?

1 When does the bank close?
2 What time did he arrive?
3 How many did he buy?
4 Where do they work?
5 How much does it cost?
6 What does she do?
7 Why did he go?
8 How did it happen?

4 Indirect questions with *if*

Make indirect questions.

Am I seeing Ms Peters next week?
Do you know if I'm seeing Ms Peters next week?

Does the plane stop in Chicago?
Do you know if the plane stops in Chicago?

1 Is the flight on time?
2 Will it take off on time?
3 Does it stop in London?
4 Did Mr Smith get on this flight?
5 Can I have a window seat?
6 Do they give you newspapers on the flight?
7 Is there a movie on the flight?

Offers

1 Offers and replies

Match the offers with the replies.

offers
1 Let me take one of your cases.
2 Would you like me to get you a coffee?
3 Shall I open a window?
4 Sit down. I'll take your coat.
5 Can I give you a hand with the washing up?
6 Why don't you let me go to the shops for you?
7 Do you need any help with photocopying those documents?

replies
A Please. It's very hot in here, isn't it?
B Thank you.
C That's very kind. I'm too busy to go myself.
D It's all right. I've nearly finished them.
E It's OK. I can manage. They aren't heavy.
F No, you stay there. I'll do it.
G No, thanks. I've just had a drink.

2 Reception

You are a receptionist for a large company. How helpful are you? What would you say to these visitors? Try to use different offer formulas for each situation.

1 'Hello. I have an appointment to see Ms Kelly at ten. I'm afraid I'm very early.'
2 'I'm sorry, I'm lost. I don't know where Miss Owen's office is.'
3 'Do I have to sign here? Sorry, I haven't got a pen.'
4 'Oh, dear. This coffee's cold.'
5 'Good morning. I have an appointment with Mr Cooper. Is there anywhere I can put my umbrella? I'm afraid it's very wet.'
6 'Oh, no! This coffee machine takes 50p pieces, and I only have pound coins.'

3 What were the offers?

Look at these replies. Can you guess what the offers were?

1 'No, thanks. I've had enough.'
2 'That's very kind of you, but I don't mind walking. It's a lovely evening.'
3 'No, don't bother. I can use this knife and fork.'
4 'If you want to, but I'm OK. It's loud enough for me already.'
5 'Yes, please. I'd love some.'

Suggestions and invitations

1 What are they saying?

Match the conversations with the pictures.

A: I'm tired of this. Let's go.
B: No, let's wait. It won't be long.

C: Shall we buy some T-shirts?
D: Certainly not. They're a waste of money.
Let's just get a programme.

E: How about parking there?
F: It's too expensive. We can park on the street.

G: Look at this! The Rolling Stones are coming to the City Hall.
H: Really? Would you like to go and see them?

I: We'll never find a space. Why don't we go back to the car park?
J: All right. Let's do that.

K: Shall we sit at the front or the back?
L: What about sitting in the middle?

2 Word order

Put these words in the correct order to make invitations.

to / you / tomorrow? / a / like / Would / see / movie
Would you like to see a movie tomorrow?

1 John's / How / party / to / going / about / tonight?
2 me? / to / Do / dinner / have / want / you / with
3 meal. / for / Let's / a / out / go
4 dance? / you / to / Would / like
5 Saturday? / come / on / you / Can / a / to / party

3 Suggestions

Make suggestions for these situations. What would you say?

1 Your class is planning an evening out together.
2 The class wants to get a birthday present for your teacher.
3 You and a friend want to practise your English.

4 Reading – Holidays or vacations?

British English is *holiday*. American English is *vacation*. True or false?

> Well, not quite true. Americans make a difference between holidays like Christmas, Easter, Independence Day, and Thanksgiving and vacations, which are once or twice a year, and are breaks from work. The British call both 'holidays'. The origin of the word is 'holy days' which means religious days or religious festivals (or national days), and the Americans still keep this meaning. In the United States, religious holidays like Christmas and Easter are not official national holidays (although most people don't work on these days), while in Britain they are. The British call all official holidays bank holidays – or days when the banks are closed. In American English you often see a definite article, *the,* before holidays. In Britain you often see a possessive adjective, such as *my, our,* or *your.*

Are these sentences true or false?

..... Americans don't use the word 'holidays'.
..... Holidays were originally religious festivals.
..... Christmas is a national holiday in the USA.
..... A vacation is a break from work.
..... Bank holidays are not official holidays.

Apologizing

1 Where can you find the signs?

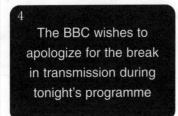

6

EXBURY PLC

Please accept our apologies for any inconvenience during building work

Match these locations with the signs.

..... on a postcard
..... inside a large public building
..... at the end of roadworks on an important road
..... on a greetings card
..... on your TV screen
..... in the doorway of a shop

2 Adjective + infinitive

Complete the spaces with these adjectives.

pleased	interesting	sorry
surprised	annoyed	difficult

1 I was very .... to hear your bad news. When will he be out of hospital?

2 I'm .... to say that you've passed your exam.

3 We were .... to meet her. We thought she was in Australia.

4 It was .... to understand the exercise, and I couldn't finish it.

5 When I collected my car from its 20,000 km service, I was very .... to find cigarette ends in the ashtray.

6 I'm looking for something .... to read.

3 Spelling: *apologise / apologize*

You will see both spellings, and both are correct. Most newspapers and publishers choose to use one spelling or the other. *The Times* newspaper, Oxford University Press, and most American dictionaries use the *-ize* spelling. The *Daily Mirror* newspaper and several British publishers prefer *-ise*. Other words like this are: *criticize, organize, recognize, sympathize.*

The following verbs always have an *-ise* spelling: *advise, advertise, practise*, promise, surprise.*
(* *practice* in American English)

Requesting permission

1 Permission

Asking for permission is always in the first person.
Can I / we …? Could I / we …? May I / we …?
Might I / we …?
We use *can / could* when we ask somebody to
do something.
Can you help me with this?
Could you pass the salt?
We don't use *may / might* when we ask
somebody to do something.

Read the notes. Which of the words in
brackets can complete the sentences?
Sometimes both words are possible.
Sometimes only one of them is possible.
Delete any words which are not correct.

1   (Can / May) I go home early tonight?
2   (Can / May) you help me?
3   (Can / May) I help you?
4   (Could / Might) I borrow your pen?
5   (Could / May) you lend me your pen?
6   (May / Might) I ask you a personal question?
7   (Can / Could) you take a message for me?
8   (Could / May) you open the door for me?

2 *Do you mind …?*

We use *Do you mind if …? / Would you mind
if …?* for asking permission.
We use *Do you mind (doing) something? /
Would you mind (doing) something?* when we
ask somebody to do something.

Look at the questions below. Write *P* if
someone is asking permission. Write *A* if they
are asking somebody to do something.

1   Do you mind if I open the window? …..
2   Would you mind opening the window? …..
3   Do you mind if I call you 'Bill'? …..
4   Would you mind carrying one of these
    bags? I can't manage both of them. …..
5   Would you mind if I turned the volume
    down? It's a bit too loud for me. …..
6   Do you mind turning your radio down?
    It's very loud. …..
7   Do you mind if I leave early? I have to
    catch a bus. …..
8   Would you mind staying later tonight? …..

3 Responses to *'Do you mind …?'* questions

Remember that the expressions we use for
responses are the same for asking permission
and asking somebody to do something. You
could reply 'Not at all' to every question in
exercise 2. Here are some possible answers to
the questions in exercise 2. Put them in the
correct boxes.

Not at all.   Actually, I do mind.
Certainly not.   Go ahead.
I'm afraid I do mind.   Yes, I do.
I'd rather you didn't.   All right.
No, I don't mind.   OK.
Actually, I do.   No.
Sorry, I do.

giving permission / agreeing to do something

refusing permission / refusing to do something

Rules and regulations

1 Dress rules

Do places have dress rules in your country?
Which places have dress rules?

Look at the four signs on the next page.
Which one is from:

a night club (or disco)?
a cruise ship?
a formal restaurant in a 5-star hotel?
a self-service café near a popular beach?

2 What do the signs mean?

Underline the correct sentences below each sign.

1

**No Shirt
No Shoes
No Service**

A You needn't wear a jacket.
B You're allowed to wear a shirt.
C Bare feet are prohibited.
D You're supposed to wear a shirt.
E You can't wear a shirt.
F You mustn't wear a shirt.
G We don't serve people without shoes.

2

**Smart
casual
clothes
please
STRICTLY
NO DENIM!**

A You must wear a suit.
B You needn't wear a tie.
C You musn't wear jeans.
D You can wear a tie if you like.
E You can't wear denim.
F You aren't allowed to wear jeans.
G You're supposed to look smart.

3

* * * *
*Gentlemen are
requested to
wear a jacket
and tie in the
Hotel Restaurant*
* * * *

A You must wear a suit.
B You can wear a tie if you like.
C You're supposed to wear a jacket.
D You may wear a jacket.
E Don't come in without a tie.
F You needn't wear a suit.
G You mustn't wear an open-necked shirt.

4

**MAPLIN'S CRUISES:
WELCOME DINNER
& DANCE IN THE
HAWAIIAN BALLROOM**

Gentlemen:
Dinner jacket
& black tie

Ladies:
Ballgown or
cocktail dress

A Men must wear a dinner jacket.
B Women may not wear trousers.
C Women mustn't wear a business suit.
D Men have to wear a tie.
E Men aren't allowed to wear a business suit.
F Women can wear a skirt and blouse.
G Casual clothes aren't permitted.

3 Questionnaire

'Let me tell you something … everyone here tonight is wearing a uniform.'
(Frank Zappa, American musician, after the blue jean-wearing audience booed the police at a rock concert.)

Choose your answers to these questions. Tick the box (✔).

1 Are you allowed to wear jeans to work / school?
   ☐ Yes
   ☐ No

2 What are you supposed to wear to work / school?
   ☐ a uniform
   ☐ formal clothes
   ☐ casual clothes
   ☐ anything I like

3 Which of these people usually wear a suit (or female equivalent) at work?
   ☐ a doctor
   ☐ a teacher
   ☐ a lawyer
   ☐ a politician
   ☐ a scientist
   ☐ a computer programmer
   ☐ a TV newsreader
   ☐ a salesperson
   ☐ a student
   ☐ a waiter

4 How do you feel about dress rules?
☐ I like to look the same as everyone else.
☐ I like to look different from everyone else.
☐ Rules are important.
☐ It doesn't matter what you wear; it's what you do that matters.

5 Are dress rules more important for men or for women?
☐ They're about the same.
☐ Rules are more important for men.
☐ Rules are more important for women.
☐ I've never thought about it.

4 Complete the spaces

Complete the spaces with these verbs.

permitted	located	supposed	allowed
reserved	accompanied		

1 Our flight attendants are pointing out the emergency exits. Emergency exits are .... at the front of the cabin and over the wings.

2 Smoking is strictly not .... in the toilets or when moving around the aircraft.

3 Passengers are .... to take one litre of duty free spirits, for example whisky, through customs.

4 Children must be .... by an adult.

5 You're .... to keep your seat belt fastened during the flight.

6 Seats can be .... forty-eight hours before the flight departs.

Saying the right thing

1 Find the different sound

All these words are from unit four. Put a ring around the word in each line which has a different underlined vowel sound.

firm	fire	worth	certainly
strict	sincere	signed	visitor
received	pleasant	colleague	accompanied
trouble	pool	rule	mood
break	memory	depth	guest
fault	waterfront	area	hall
smoking	policy	home	Skydome
museum	use	usually	loud
lost	Ontario	job	post

2 Compound words

Match the words in the first column with words in the second column. All the words are from unit four. Match each word once only, and match all of them.

changing	store
tea	director
sales	officer
managing	room
security	space
parking	directory
phone	representative
department	break

3 What would you say?

Here are some more situations like the ones in the Student's Book. What would you say?

1 You're at an information bureau in a tourist town. You want to know where the museum is. What do you say?
A 'Where's the museum?'
B 'Can you tell me where the museum is?'
C 'Hello. I wonder if you can help me. I'm looking for the museum.'

2 You're in a restaurant with a friend. A stranger is opposite you, and has ketchup on their chin. What would you do?
A Nothing.
B Nudge your friend and point.
C Say, 'Excuse me, you've got some ketchup on your chin.'

3 Someone has just parked their car across a pedestrian crossing. What would you do?
   A It's not my business. I wouldn't do anything.
   B Walk over, and tell them politely that parking is not allowed on pedestrian crossings in your town.
   C Call a police officer.

Look at the **scoring** section on page 136 in the Student's Book. What scores would you give the answers?

After you've finished

Skills check

Imagine you are the speaker in these situations. What do you say?

place	speaker	function
the street	a stranger	ask for directions
restaurant	customer	order a drink
office	co-worker	ask to borrow some money
school	student	ask permission to leave early
school	teacher	ask a student to close the door
party	guest	apologize for arriving late
customer's home	repair person	ask to use the customer's phone
on the phone	a friend	suggest a good place for lunch

Grammar check

You can test yourself. Choose the correct word.

1 Do you know where (can I / I can) park?
2 Can you tell me if (there is / is there) a rest room in this building?
3 I don't know what time (is it / it is).
4 (Will / Would / Do) you like to take a seat?
5 I'll get you a drink (during / when / while) you're waiting.
6 It's raining hard. Let ('s / is / we) take a taxi.
7 I'm thirsty. (Will / Shall / Do) we stop and get a drink?
8 (I'm / I / I've) afraid that it's all my fault.
9 Sorry. I promise it (wouldn't / doesn't / won't) happen again.
10 Do you mind if I open the window? (Yes / Not) at all. I'm hot, too.
11 Am I (allow / allowing / allowed) to leave my car here?
12 You (aren't supposed / mustn't / shouldn't) to copy video tapes.
13 You (aren't allowed / mustn't / are forbidden) smoke on the London Underground.
14 Excuse me, I (think / suppose / wonder) if you can direct me to the nearest station?
15 May I ask you a question? (Of course / Not at all / Yes, you probably may.)
16 Could I (possibly / probably / certainly) borrow your pen?
17 She (can / may / could) speak when she was one year old.
18 *Will you pass the salt?* is a (question about the future / request / suggestion).
19 *Be, do,* and *have* are (auxiliary / modal) verbs.
20 *It might happen* means something is (certain / probable / possible).

UNIT FIVE
Conversation strategies

Thinking about learning

Working alone or with others

Do you learn best by working on your own, or by working co-operatively with other people? React to these statements about classroom activities in your English lessons. In each case write down your response: *A* (A is closest to my feelings), *B* (B is closest to my feelings), or *X* (I have no preference).

1 .....
A I enjoy working by myself.
B I'm not very good at working by myself.

2 .....
A When I work by myself, I can concentrate better.
B When I work by myself I often feel bored.

3 .....
A When I do activities in class with other students I don't learn very much.
B When I do activities in class with other students I find it more interesting.

4 .....
A In role-plays I try to practise the grammar and vocabulary we've studied during the lesson.
B In role-plays I think about communicating with the other students. I don't think much about grammar or vocabulary.

5 .....
A I like to organize my own learning and revision.
B I like the teacher to tell me what I need to learn and revise.

6 .....
A When I have homework or a project, I don't want to discuss it with anyone.
B When I have homework or a project, I like to discuss it with other students.

7 .....
A I like to choose the exercises and activities from the course book which are most useful for me.
B I am happy with the sequence of the course book and the activities.

Scoring

More 'A's than 'B's:
Independent learner
You learn best when you are controlling your own learning. You know what you want to learn and how you are going to learn it.
More 'B's than 'A's:
Co-operative learner
You learn best when you are co-operating with other people in the class. You like the teacher to organize your learning.
A lot of 'X's:
Balanced learner
You are well-balanced and happy with a variety of activities.

While you are working on unit five, think about the activities. Note them, and for each activity say whether it is more useful for independent learners or for co-operative learners. Say whether you enjoyed each activity and whether you learned from it.

Topics of conversation

1 Frequency adverbs

Complete the spaces with frequency adverbs, so that the sentences are true for you.

1 I .... talk about work during meals.

2 I .... discuss politics with my friends.

3 I .... talk about sport.

4 I .... discuss relationships with people at work / school.

5 I .... speak to my neighbours.

6 I .... talk about rock music.

7 I .... discuss my family with colleagues.

2 Asking questions

I've been to the bank today. (When?)
When did you go?

Write past simple questions.

1 I've lost my book. (Where?)
2 I've already had my lunch. (What time?)
3 She's just bought a new watch. (Where?)
4 They've met Princess Diana. (When?)
5 We've already seen *Waterworld II*. (When?)
6 He's hurt his arm badly. (How?)

3 Word square

Find the past participles in this word square.

```
G  Y  G  F  A  L  L  E  N  S
Z  L  O  O  H  E  O  B  I  W
W  O  N  U  A  F  S  J  M  U
B  E  E  N  D  T  T  B  K  M
R  U  N  D  R  I  V  E  N  W
O  X  L  S  H  U  T  G  O  T
U  U  E  A  H  I  T  U  W  O
G  A  T  T  A  K  E  N  N  L
H  G  I  V  E  N  A  R  U  D
T  H  O  U  G  H  T  M  E  T
```

Women and men

1 Adverbs: frequency, manner, and degree

Adverbs of frequency tell us how often
something happens.
Adverbs of manner tell us how something
happens.
Adverbs of degree make a following adjective
stronger or weaker.

What kind of adverbs are the underlined
words below? Write *F* (frequency), *M*
(manner), or *D* (degree).

1 I generally get up late at weekends. .....
2 These shoes are slightly too small for me. .....
3 I'm rather worried about my job. .....
4 She drives carefully. .....
5 Do you normally have coffee with your
   breakfast? .....
6 They answered several of the questions
   incorrectly. .....
7 Yes, it's quite nice. I'll have one. .....
8 He is frequently late for work. .....
9 She sings well. .....

2 Word order (1)

Match the two parts of the sentences.

1 Frequency adverbs usually come …
2 Adverbs of manner usually come …
3 Adverbs of degree usually come …

A ..... before an adjective.
B ..... before the verb, but after the verb 'to be'.
C ..... after the verb.

3 Word order (2)

Rewrite these sentences in the correct order.

ever / He / exercise. / any / takes / hardly
He hardly ever takes any exercise.

1 annoyed. / was / quite / feeling / She
2 normally / early. / I / get up
3 hot. / coffee / This / very / is
4 badly. / goalkeeper / played / The
5 late / We / rarely / are / work. / for
6 slowly? / could / speak / you / Please /
   more

4 Comparison of adverbs

There have been several surveys about
people's behaviour in cities and in small
towns or in villages. What do you think the
results of the survey were? Underline the
answers (the correct answers are at the
bottom of this page).

1 People in large cities walk (more quickly /
   less quickly) than people in small towns.
2 People in small towns speak (more slowly /
   more quickly) than people in cities.
3 People in small towns stand (closer
   together / further apart) than people in
   cities.
4 People in cities speak (more quietly /
   louder) than people in small towns.
5 People in small towns drive (more
   carefully / more carelessly) than people in
   cities.

Answers: 1 more quickly **2** more slowly **3** further apart
4 louder **5** more carefully

5 Adverbs of degree

Adverbs of degree (also called adverbs of completeness) are a type of qualifier. Look at these sentences. Is the <u>underlined</u> adverb making the following adjective stronger (+) or weaker (−)?

1 I'm feeling <u>extremely</u> tired. .....
2 He was <u>rather</u> angry. .....
3 It's <u>quite</u> big. .....
4 She was <u>terribly</u> worried. .....
5 My car was <u>slightly</u> damaged. .....
6 This machine is <u>completely</u> useless. .....
7 Sorry, I'm <u>a bit</u> early. .....
8 I was <u>kind of</u> nervous about the interview. .....
9 It's <u>almost</u> dark. .....
10 That's <u>totally</u> wrong. .....

6 Travelling by air

Scottish International Airways gives this advice to travellers.

✈ Scottish International Airways

How to minimize jet lag and cross the Atlantic in comfort.

- Wear loose, comfortable clothes.
- Take off your shoes.
- Don't eat too much.
- Be careful with alcohol! Don't drink too much.
- Drink plenty of water – long distance flights dehydrate you.
- Set your watch to the time zone of your destination.
- Try to get some sleep – we provide eye masks in our Welcome packs.
- If you don't want to be woken for meals, place the sticker DON'T WAKE FOR MEALS on the back of the seat in front of you.

Give advice to someone who is going on a long flight. Write sentences beginning:

You should ...
You shouldn't ...

7 Welcome packs

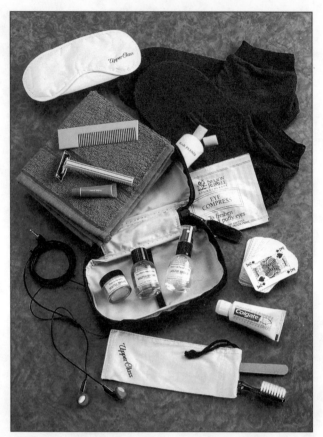

Most airlines provide Welcome packs for passengers. This is what you get on Scottish International Airways.

Economy Class:	plastic bag, socks, eye mask, headphones
First Class:	leather bag, slippers, eye mask, stereo headphones, razor, shaving cream, toothbrush, toothpaste, mouthwash, cosmetics, perfume, after-shave, comb, shoehorn, key-ring
Children:	headphones, comic, drawing book, coloured pencils, postcard, playing cards **plus** (First Class) electronic game, travel Monopoly

Scottish International Airways are introducing a new Business Class. Tickets will cost more than Economy but less than First Class. What should they put in the Business Class pack? They have decided to have different packs for male and female travellers. Make two lists.

Attentive listening

1 Pronunciation

Look at the words for noises in the first box. Circle the word in the second box which has a different vowel sound.

1	2			
er...	sir	car	her	girl
uh ...	but	cut	cute	nut
ah...	pair	far	hard	father
um ...	some	home	thumb	come
eh?	may	plate	than	wait
oh!	so	note	coat	do
ooh!	out	you	blue	food

2 Write an exercise

Write an exercise like the one above. You need to think of three words with the same vowel sound and one with a different vowel sound. In your next class, you can ask another student to do your exercise.

1	2
like	
will	
could	
phone	
tell	
call	

3 The meaning of sounds

Which of the expressions (1–6) can you use to replace the underlined sounds (A–F)?

1 This is a surprise.
2 I hear you.
3 Let me think.
4 Pardon?
5 This is nice.
6 Now I understand.

A Eh? What did you say?
B Ah, so this is the switch that turns it on!
C Oh! I didn't expect to see you here today.
D Ooh! Chocolate cake! My favourite!
E The answer's ... um ... 3,465.
F Uh-huh, ... uh-huh ... then what did you do?

☛ If you need help, look back at *Making the right noises* in unit two of the Student's Book.

4 Noises in your language

What noises do people use in your language during conversations?
Do different noises have different meanings?
List some noises from your language and their meanings (in English!).

Conversation fillers

1 Expected responses and disagreement

Sometimes we want to check that the listener is paying attention to us. We can use question tags. When a speaker uses question tags, they expect the listener to agree with them. Normally, it is polite for the listener to give the expected response.

☛ see also *Checking information* in unit three.

Look at this table.

The weather	It's a nice day, isn't it?
	It wasn't very nice yesterday, was it?
	It rained hard this morning, didn't it?
	It's been a cold winter, hasn't it?
	You don't know what weather to expect, do you?
	It won't rain today, will it?
Expected response	Yes, it is. / Yes. / Mmm.
	No, it wasn't. / No.
	Yes, it did. / Yes.
	Yes, it has. / Yeah, right.
	No, you don't. / No.
	No, it won't. / I don't think so.
Disagreement	Do you think so? I don't.
	It was OK.
	It wasn't too bad.
	It's been all right.
	I think it'll stay nice.
	I disagree. I think it will.

When you are using question tags you can't say anything controversial (things the listener might disagree with).

'Your president's an idiot, isn't she?'
'The food in your country's terrible, isn't it?'
'Young people are awful these days, aren't they?'

Look at these topics. Make sentences about each topic with question tags.

1 A TV programme

2 Politics

3 Music

4 Diet

5 A sport

6 Art

2 Deletion

When people are speaking, they don't always make complete sentences. They leave some words out. This is called *deletion*. In *Conversation fillers* in the Student's Book the taxi driver left some words out.

Beautiful day, isn't it?
It's a beautiful day, isn't it?

Too many tourists.
There are too many tourists.

Complete these sentences in the same way.

1 A lot of traffic, isn't there?
2 Too many cars.
3 Cold this morning, wasn't it?
4 Bad news on the radio, wasn't there?
5 Always bad news nowadays.
6 Going to the station, are you?
7 Waterloo Station, wasn't it?
8 Not enough trains, are there?

3 Responding

When people use question tags, they expect the listener to agree. It's unusual to disagree with a statement with a question tag. Look at the table in exercise 1 and write responses which agree with the speaker.

1 There are too many cars, aren't there?
2 There aren't enough buses, are there?
3 You can't get taxis at this time of day, can you?
4 You won't walk home, will you?
5 You'll take the underground, won't you?
6 It was cold this morning, wasn't it?
7 There weren't any calls for me, were there?

Pausing

1 Types of punctuation

Put the punctuation marks next to the words below.

? . , : ; ' ' * ( ) – / !

..... comma
..... period (USA) / full stop (UK)
..... question mark
..... exclamation mark
..... quotes (USA) / inverted commas (UK)
..... dash
..... parentheses (USA) / brackets (UK)
..... colon
..... semi-colon
..... slash
..... asterisk

2 Capital letters

Rewrite these sentences with capital letters in the correct places.

1 vancouver is the biggest city in british columbia.
2 her husband's name is john and they live in walton street in oxford.
3 people in new york city speak more quickly than people in alaska.
4 we know two people called diana and they both live in england.
5 it was a wonderful holiday and we saw the river ganges, the taj mahal, mount everest, and the indian ocean.

3 Commas

Say the sentences aloud to yourself. Think whether they need commas, and where the commas should be. If you can say something without pausing at all, it probably doesn't need a comma.

1 Alaska is a beautiful state but it's cold in the winter.
2 He spoke slowly carefully and thoughtfully.
3 The Beatles were John Paul George and Ringo.
4 She doesn't like me my brother my sister or any of my family.
5 My address is 35 Sloane Street Chelsea London SW3 4RU England.

4 Vocabulary

Complete the spaces with these verbs. Use each verb once only.

paused	responded	hesitated
stopped	interrupted	

1 The speaker .... , sat down, and drank a glass of water.
2 It was an embarrassing question, and he .... before replying.
3 The speaker .... for a moment while the audience thought about what she had said, then she continued.
4 Someone .... the speaker to ask a question.
5 The speaker .... angrily to the question.

Thinking time

1 *You want to know what I think?*

We often use indirect questions when we are hesitating.

Question:
What do you think about this?

Repeating the question indirectly:
You want to know what I think about this? or
You're asking me what I think about this? or
You want me to say what I think about this?

Complete the indirect questions (IQ).

1 Q   Where did you leave it?

   IQ   You want to know .... ?

2 Q   Who did you give the information to ?

   IQ   You're asking me .... ?

3 Q   When did you see it?

   IQ   You want me to tell you .... ?

4 Q   What do you know about this problem?

   IQ   You want us to say .... ?

5 Q   Where did you go yesterday?

   IQ   You'd like to know .... ?

2 *You want to know if …?*

 Q   Do you believe in Father Christmas?
IQ   *You're asking me if I believe in Father Christmas?*

Complete the indirect questions.

1 Q   Do you know the time?

   IQ   You want to know if .... ?

2 Q   Is Baker Street in London?

   IQ   You're asking me if .... ?

3 Q   Was that your car in the car park?

   IQ   You'd like to know if .... ?

4 Q   Did you leave work early last night?

   IQ   You want me to tell you if ....

            .... ?

5 Q   Have you finished the job yet?

   IQ   You're asking me if .... ?

3 Conversation

Complete the spaces in this conversation. Use as many hesitation devices as possible (see the Student's Book).

TEACHER: Can you explain Einstein's Theory of Relativity, please?

STUDENT: .... ?

TEACHER: I said, can you explain Einstein's Theory of Relativity?

STUDENT: ....
.... ?

TEACHER: That's right.

STUDENT: ....

TEACHER: Go on.

STUDENT: .... Do you want the general theory or the special theory?

Being diplomatic

1 Compound words

Match the words in the first column with words in the second column. All the words are from this section in the Student's Book. Match each word once only, and match all of them.

heart	results
test	home
first	lottery
old people's	manager
bank	prize
national	attack

2 Matching

Match the words in the first column with words in the second column. All the words are from this section in the Student's Book. Match each word once only, and match all of them.

win	to attention
get	dead
break	the calculations
do	diplomatic
drop	to the point
overdraw	a prize
stand	the news
be	an account

3 Choose the best sentences

What did they actually say? Look at the underlined adverbs of manner, then choose the best sentences.

1 The police officer spoke <u>quietly and sympathetically.</u>
   A Your dog ran in front of a truck.
   B I'm afraid there's been an accident.
   C Your dog's dead.

2 The manager was furious! He spoke <u>angrily</u> without trying to be diplomatic.
   A Right! That's it! You're fired!
   B Please sit down. I'm sorry, but I have some rather bad news.
   C I wonder if we could talk about your future with the company.

3 The doctor decided to get straight to the point, and she spoke <u>clearly and directly.</u>
   A I don't know how to say this, but I think we're going to need to investigate your problem a little further.
   B How's your new job? By the way, I think I'm going to need to do some tests on you.
   C You're going to need an operation.

4 He had crashed into a colleague's empty car in the car park, and he wanted to break the news <u>gently</u> and to speak <u>diplomatically.</u>
   A Hello. I just crashed straight into your car.
   B You know there isn't much space in that car park, and there have been a lot of minor accidents, don't you? Well, …
   C You know you cleaned and polished your car yesterday? Well, it was a waste of time.

Turn-taking

1 Matching

Match the sentences (1–7) with their purposes (A–G).

sentence

1 Actually, that isn't the main point here.
2 Excuse me, I haven't finished.
3 I think other people want to give their ideas on this.
4 Let's go back to the point.
5 If I can just say something here …
6 What's your opinion, Frank?
7 Absolutely.

purpose

A stopping someone interrupting
B choosing the next speaker
C keeping to the point
D telling someone they're not keeping to the point
E showing you're listening attentively
F stopping someone dominating
G trying to interrupt

2 *too* and *very*

Choose the best word to complete the sentences.

1 Look, those apples are (too / very) cheap. Let's buy some.
2 No, I don't want that shirt. It's (too / very) small for me.
3 I'm (too / very) angry with her.
4 Be careful, it's (too / very) hot to eat! You'll burn your mouth!
5 He's going to have a rest. He's (too / very) tired.
6 Phew! It's 40°C outside. It's much (too / very) hot to play tennis.
7 More ice, please. I like lemonade when it's (too / very) cold.

3 *stop doing / stop to do*

Sarah was working on her computer. Suddenly the phone rang.

What did she stop doing?
She stopped working on her computer.

What did she stop to do?
She stopped to answer the phone.

Write similar questions and answers for these situations.

A Paul was driving to London. He saw a petrol station, and turned off the motorway because he needed some petrol.

B Mr and Mrs Carter were walking along the beach. Mr Carter was thirsty. Mrs Carter saw a kiosk which was selling ice-cream and soft drinks.

Interrupting

Silvia is paying by credit card. The shop assistant put the credit card through the machine, and the credit card company has asked the shop to telephone them. Complete the spaces using the expressions below.

Wait a moment.	May I say something?
Sorry, but …	Do you mind if I speak to them?
Actually, …	Please let me speak to them.
	Can I interrupt you?

ASSISTANT: Hello? This is Lewis Jones plc. Yes, the customer is with me. Yes, that's right, Miss Scott is here.

SILVIA: …………, it's Mrs Scott.

ASSISTANT: Right. …………. I'll just ask her. (to Silvia) It's a routine check. They want to know your date of birth.

SILVIA: This is ridiculous. I don't know …

ASSISTANT: She doesn't know.

SILVIA: …………, ………… I didn't finish. I don't know why they're asking.

ASSISTANT: They're just checking that it's your credit card.

SILVIA: All right. It's the 14th of February.

ASSISTANT: The 14th of February. Yes, I know. I see. Yes, I understand.

SILVIA: .... ?

ASSISTANT: Sorry?

SILVIA: .... ?

ASSISTANT: She wants to speak to you. No, I know. We've had a lot of problems recently, too. Yes, we …

SILVIA: .... ?

ASSISTANT: Oh, yes, of course. Sorry, madam. What is it?

SILVIA: .... ?

ASSISTANT: Oh, yes. All right. Here's the phone.

SILVIA: Good afternoon. This is Mrs Scott. Now, what seems to be the problem?

After you've finished

Skills check

Conversation checklist

When you start talking to someone, what conversation strategies do you use? Look through the checklist and tick Yes or No.

Conversation strategy	Yes	No
Do you start a conversation with a positive comment?	☐	☐
Do you try to find a topic that interests both of you?	☐	☐
Do you avoid topics that might be offensive?	☐	☐
Do you talk about yourself all the time?	☐	☐
Do you ask questions?	☐	☐
Do you avoid personal questions?	☐	☐
Do you interrupt the other person frequently?	☐	☐
Do you show that you are listening attentively?	☐	☐
Do you watch the other person's body language, so that you know whether you are boring them?	☐	☐

Grammar check

You can test yourself. Choose the correct word.

1 Who have you (speaking / speak / spoken) to today?
2 What did you (spoke / spoken / speak) about?
3 She drives more (carefully / careful) than him.
4 Which one is talking more (loud / louder / loudly)?
5 They (should / ought / had better) to ban cyclists from busy roads.
6 It often rains in London, (don't / isn't / doesn't) it?
7 I don't know. It (is depending / depend / depends) on the situation.
8 Please stop (interrupt / to interrupt / interrupting) me. I haven't finished yet.
9 Please (let / let's / to let) me finish.
10 Do you mind (if / when / that) I say something?
11 I'm afraid I've (yet / just / immediately) had some bad news.
12 She isn't here. She's (been / gone) to Australia to live.
13 You (ought not / shouldn't / had better not) allow people to interrupt.
14 You were here yesterday, (wasn't it? / weren't you? / didn't you?)
15 People in big cities walk and talk (most quickly / quickly / more quickly) than people from small towns.
16 I'm afraid you ('ll / must / ought) have to speak to the boss about this.
17 It's an excellent job! Well (do! / did! / done!)
18 *Do you know what it is?* is (a direct / an echo / an indirect) question.
19 *Quickly* is (a verb / an adverb / an adjective).
20 *Hardly ever* is (a frequency adverb / an adverb of manner / a time word).

Thinking about learning

Exercise types

There are six language exercises below. Do them as quickly as you can.

Exercise 1

Choose the correct answers.

1 I thought the movie was pretty ....

   A bored   B bores me   C boring   D to bore

2 He was really .... when he heard the news.

   A worries B worried C worrying D to worry

Exercise 2

Read this extract from a story.

> He walked in and found a seat. A waiter arrived and he ordered an ale. It was a hot day and he felt like a long drink after the walk from Seaford. The ale wasn't cold enough for him, but he was thirsty and so he drank it anyway.

Do you want to stop and look up *ale* in the dictionary, or are you happy to continue reading without getting a definition of *ale*?

Exercise 3

Complete the spaces with *was, wasn't, were,* or *weren't.*

Two women .... walking along a country road. One of them .... wearing an old hat, and the other .... carrying an umbrella, although it .... raining. They .... talking to each other, they .... walking in silence.

Exercise 4

In this text, every tenth word is missing. Can you think of words to complete the spaces?

Suddenly Jake woke up. He could hear a strange .... He was terrified! He quickly climbed out of bed .... went to the window. The moon was shining in .... sky and there were no clouds. Jake could see .... clearly. Just across the street there was a large .... animal walking slowly along the pavement. It was the .... again.

Exercise 5

Put the words below into three groups: 1 – colours 2 – materials 3 – items of clothing.

sock	wool	grey	jeans
hat	green	yellow	nylon
pink	tights	red	purple
blouse	plastic	leather	cotton
T-shirt	brown	denim	blue

Exercise 6

How many words can you add to this word network? You can add extra branches if you like.

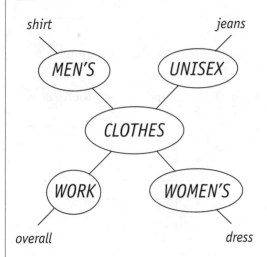

Assess the exercises

Think about the types of exercise you've just done. Assess the exercise type (not the particular exercise) on the chart below. Tick the appropriate boxes.

Exercise	1	2	3	4	5	6
I used my knowledge of rules.						
I used my imagination and made guesses.						
There was more than one correct answer.						
This was a good way of organizing information.						
I could see the point of the exercise.						

Some learners like to see logic, structure, and organization. They prefer exercises like 1, 3, and 5. They're often unhappy with exercises where there is more than one possible answer.

Other learners don't need to understand every word. They prefer exercises like 2, 4, and 6. They're happy to guess and to use their imagination. We all need to learn in both ways.

Ways of presenting information

1 Word study

Look at the chart. You can *tell* a story. You can *explain* a story to someone who doesn't understand it or who hasn't read it. You can *talk about* a story that you have read. You can't *give* a story and you don't *describe* a story. Put ticks and crosses for the other words on the chart.

	give	tell	explain	talk about	describe
a story	✗	✔	✔	✔	✗
a joke					
a process					
information					
instructions					
a lecture					
something					
someone					

2 Choose the verb

Complete the spaces with one of these verbs.

said	told	asked	explained
described	talked	gave	

1 He .... the thief to a police officer, who took notes. Then they looked at some photos.

2 The instruction book .... how to change the LaserWriter cartridge.

3 She invited me into the office and .... me if I would like a cup of tea.

4 He .... me to be quiet, and to listen carefully.

5 I .... , 'I'm very sorry.'

6 He .... about his holiday, then asked me about my last holiday.

7 She .... a short lecture about nuclear physics.

Explaining something

1 Reading activity

First write down the numbers from one to sixteen in a table like this:

1	2	3	4
5	6	7	8
9	10	11	12
13	14	15	16

Choose a number and circle it. Then cross out all the numbers in the same row. Then cross out all the numbers in the same column. For example, if you circled 7, you cross out 5, 6, 8 (same row), and 3, 11, and 15 (same column).

Circle another number that has not yet been crossed out. Then cross out the other numbers in the same column and the same row.

Circle a third number. Cross out any numbers in the same column and row.

There will only be one number left. Circle it.

Add up the four circled numbers. The answer will be 34.

When you try this puzzle with someone, begin by writing 34 on a piece of paper and folding the paper. Don't show them the paper until they have finished the puzzle.

2   Find the different sound

Put a ring around the word in each line which has a different <u>underlined</u> vowel sound. All the words are from unit six.

p<u>ie</u>ce	s<u>e</u>quence	l<u>e</u>cture	<u>ea</u>sy
c<u>o</u>rner	gr<u>ou</u>p	f<u>o</u>rmal	jigs<u>aw</u>
p<u>u</u>zzle	<u>u</u>pside	c<u>o</u>lour	t<u>u</u>rn
compl<u>e</u>te	id<u>e</u>ntify	<u>e</u>dge	<u>e</u>ver
l<u>o</u>gical	b<u>o</u>x	f<u>o</u>llow	bel<u>ow</u>
l<u>a</u>rge	expl<u>ai</u>n	st<u>a</u>ges	w<u>ay</u>s

Giving instructions

1   *when, before, after,* etc.

Choose the correct word.

1   Drivers should signal (when / before / after) they turn a corner.
2   Passengers mustn't use the toilets (as soon as / before / while) the train is in the station.
3   You shouldn't go swimming (after / before / while) you've had a large meal.
4   Waiters aren't allowed to smoke (before / until / when) they're serving customers.
5   In Britain people can't drive (after / until / while) they're seventeen.
6   We apologize for the delay. We'll take off (before / while / as soon as) we get permission from air traffic control.

2   When do you do these things?

Write six complete sentences about your daily routines using these words.

when   while   before   after   as soon as   until

*I have dinner **as soon as** I get home.*
*I eat my breakfast **before** I get dressed.*
*I usually wash my hair **while** I'm having a shower.*

☛ There will be more work on *when, before, after,* etc. in **Language Focus 7** in the Student's Book.

3   Opposites

Complete the spaces with words opposite in meaning to the underlined words.

1   Take <u>deep</u> breaths. Don't take .... breaths.
2   <u>Raise</u> your arms, then .... your arms.
3   Your voice will sound <u>deep</u>. It won't sound ....
4   You'll feel <u>relaxed.</u> You won't feel ....
5   The exercises aren't <u>difficult.</u> They're ....

Describing a sequence

1   How to use a card phone in Britain

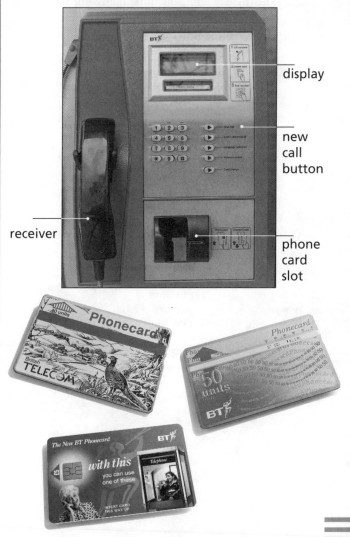

display

new call button

receiver

phone card slot

Number these instructions in the correct order from 1 to 7.

..... If you want to make a further call, do not replace the receiver. Just press the new call button.

..... Next dial the number and wait for a connection.

..... Secondly insert a BT phonecard, with the green side up and in the direction of the arrows on the card. Some BT phones will accept credit cards as well as phone cards. Insert a credit card with the black stripe on the right and away from you, and slide it through.

..... Finally, don't forget to remove your phone card after you have finished.

..... The display will show how many units are left on the card. The minimum charge is one unit.

..... First lift the receiver and wait for a dialling tone.

..... When your phone card runs out of units you will hear a bleeping noise. To continue the call, remove it and insert a new card.

2 Matching

Match the verbs in the first column with verbs with the same meaning in the second column.

emerge	put into
remove	put back
insert	take out
replace	pick up
uses all of	runs out of
lift	come out

3 Developing vocabulary

Read this text.

We use strange words for phones. We still use the verb *dialling* even though most modern phones are *touchtone* phones, i.e. they have *keypads,* not *dials.* Maybe a better word would be *inputting* as with computers, or *keying in* which means the same thing. A *receiver* receives sounds, but we call the piece you hold a receiver even though it sends sounds as well as receiving them. Then there are those *buttons,* # and *. The # symbol is called a *hash sign* in Britain and a *pound sign* in America. Why a pound sign? On a British typewriter or computer keyboard, the symbol £ is on the same *key* as 3, SHIFT-3. On an American keyboard you get a # instead of £. In the USA the # symbol has been used for years, meaning number, as in #24, and this use is growing in Britain, replacing the abbreviation *no.* for number. Modern phones also use the # key before a number. *Recorded messages* might say 'For the marketing department, press the pound sign then number 25', or 'press pound 25'. The * sign is called an *asterisk* in punctuation, but on phones it's more often called a *star.*

Symbols on computer keyboards:
Britain: SHIFT-3 = £   OPTION-3 = #
USA: SHIFT-3 = #   OPTION-3 = £

Look at the words in *italic*. How many of them are new for you?

Looking at facts and figures

1 Points and commas

How would you say these numbers?

6.725 *six point seven two five*
6,725 *six thousand seven hundred and twenty-five*

Write these numbers in words.

1.75	....	560,000	....
2,941	....	2.95	....
1,500,000	....	17.5	....
11,748	....	12.33	....

In writing we use commas for thousands, tens of thousands, hundreds of thousands, and millions. Computer programs which calculate do not recognize a comma (or any other punctuation except a decimal point) in numbers. The only punctuation on a calculator is the decimal point. In handwriting, we often place the decimal point higher – 45·3, 3·987.

2 Fractions

How would you say these fractions?

1/4	*a quarter*
2/3	*two thirds*
5/7	*five sevenths*

Write these fractions in words.

3/4	....	1/3	....
2/5	....	5/6	....
4/7	....	3/8	....
8/9	....	7/10	....

3 Arithmetic

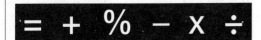

Write the signs for these words.

1	..... plus	4	..... minus
2	..... multiplication	5	..... division
3	..... equals	6	..... percentage

4 Matching

Match the words in the first column with words with the same meaning in the second column.

five minus two	divide five by two
five times two	add two to five
five plus two	multiply five by two
five over two	take away two from five

5 *was doing / did*

Choose the correct verbs.

1 Twenty thousand fans (waited / were waiting) when the rock group (were arriving / arrived) at the stadium.

2 He (cut / was cutting) himself while he (was shaving / shaved).

3 I (was sitting / sat) in my garden when the earthquake (started / was starting). It (was measuring / measured) 7.3 on the Richter scale.

4 The bus (was travelling / travelled) along the M25 motorway when the accident (was happening / happened).

5 They (had / were having) breakfast when their friends (phoned / were phoning).

☞ See the Student's Book, **Language Focus 6**, exercises 3, 4, and 5 for more work on these tenses.

6 Times

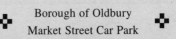

Borough of Oldbury
Market Street Car Park

PARKING TICKET

DO NOT LEAVE TICKET IN VEHICLE
TAKE TO PAY MACHINE BEFORE DEPARTING

One hour: 40p   Two hours: 90p
Two to three hours: £1.50

MAXIMUM STAY THREE HOURS

| ARRIVAL TIME | DEPARTURE TIME | PARKING FEE |
| 13.56 | 15.59 | £ 1.50 |

Look at the ticket and complete the spaces in the sentences with these words.

| after | before | between |
| for | just before | at |

1 The car was parked .... more than two hours.

2 It arrived .... 13.56.

3 It left .... four o'clock.

4 It was in the car park .... 13.56 and 15.59.

5 The fee would be 90p if the car left .... 15.56.

6 Unfortunately, it left .... 15.59, so the driver had to pay for three hours.

Presenting facts and figures

1 Talking about graphs

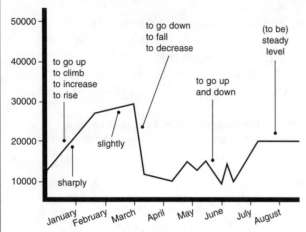

Look at the graph. Match words in the first circle with their opposites in the second circle. Be careful to match part of speech and tense.

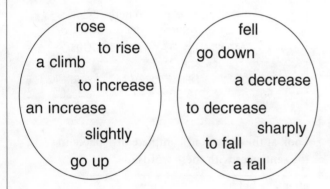

2 Signalling

Put these signals into the correct sections of the table. Some of them may fit into more than one section. You may want to copy the table.

Finally…   Last of all …
First …   Next …
The next thing is …   One example of this is …
For example …   Let's look at …
My topic is …   One example is …
Let's turn to …   To sum up …
In conclusion …   After that …
The chart shows …   As you can see …
I'd like to talk about …   The subject of this talk is …

Introduction
Sequencing
Changing
Giving examples / showing pictures
Conclusions

3 Disappearing animals

This is a transcript of a short talk about the North American passenger pigeon. The signals are missing. Complete the blanks with signals of your choice.

'………… the North American passenger pigeon. Two hundred years ago this bird made up approximately forty per cent of the bird population of North America.

………… , what was this bird like?

………… at the picture.

………… from the picture it was a beautiful bird about thirty centimetres long, and it was long-lived. Many birds lived for twenty-five years. It could fly at ninety-five kilometres per hour and could travel 1500 kilometres in a day.

In 1813 the artist James Audobon saw a flock of passenger pigeons in Kentucky. The flock was one and a half kilometres wide, and took nearly three hours to pass over him. He estimated that there had been just over one billion (1,000,000,000) birds in the flock. Several other flocks followed in the next few days.

………… what happened to the birds. They were hunted for meat. In 1878 thousands of hunters attacked a flock in Michigan. The flock was on the ground in an area fifty kilometres long by eight kilometres wide. Around a billion birds were destroyed. By 1896, after forty years of intensive hunting, only about 250,000 birds remained.

.... , in 1900, the last wild passenger pigeon was killed in Ohio. The last of the species, a 29-year-old bird called Martha, died in Cincinnati Zoo on the first of September 1914. The species was extinct.

.... , the largest species of bird in North America had been completely destroyed in approximately one hundred years.'

4 Find words which mean:

1 a large group of birds
2 calculated, guessed
3 look for and kill animals for food
4 (of an animal) not in a zoo, not domestic
5 (of a species) dead, gone

5 Approximations

Look back through the text, and underline the words which mean 'approximately'.

6 Writing

Use the notes and write a short speech about another North American bird, the Carolina Parakeet.

The Carolina Parakeet

Only parrot native to the USA. Lived in forests in east of USA. Early 19th century – many parakeets. 30 cm long, green and yellow body and tail, orange and yellow head, red and orange wings.

Hunted. Why?
1) as a cage bird / pet
2) for feathers
3) Farms replaced forests. Parakeets ate seeds, fruit, grain, so farmers killed them.

1880 – very few remained.
1904 – last time a parakeet was seen in the wild.
1914 – last one died in Cincinnati Zoo – two weeks after the last passenger pigeon, in a cage only fifteen metres away.

This is just one example. Many species have become extinct. Many are in danger of extinction.

---

7 Optional: record yourself

Record your speech on a cassette. Listen to yourself. Do you sound interesting?

You can record yourself frequently. You can note new vocabulary or expressions on a cassette.

Narrating

1 The past perfect

I was tired because (I / not / sleep well).
I was tired because I hadn't slept well.

Put the words in brackets into the past perfect.

1 When we got there (the party / already / begin).
2 He was talking to a man who (just / return / from Africa).
3 I saw my cousin yesterday. (I / not / see her / for two years).
4 They weren't thirsty because (they / just / have / a drink).
5 I went to Niagara Falls last year. (I / never / be / to Canada / before).
6 The referee sent the defender off the field because (he / kick / the other team's striker).
7 Sorry I was rude yesterday. When you phoned (I / just / start / my dinner).
8 She rented a car during her first visit to Britain. She was nervous because (she / not / drive / on the left / before).

2 Past simple or past perfect?

Put one verb in each sentence into the past simple and the other into the past perfect.

1 I (run) to the shop, but when I got there it (already / close).
2 When we (get) to the station the train (already / leave).
3 I (watch) the TV film for an hour before I realized that I (see) it before.
4 I (not / listen) to his story because I (hear) it before.
5 She (win) a million dollars before they (ask) her to leave the casino.
6 He (know) California well because he (be) there several times before.

3   Past time expressions

Number these past time expressions in order
from 1 (nearest to now) to 8 (furthest from
now).

..... a few hours ago
..... last week
..... the day before yesterday
..... a couple of hours ago
..... the week before last
..... yesterday
..... three days ago
..... in the last few minutes

4   Verb forms

Complete this table.

infinitive	present participle	past tense	past participle
to talk	talking		
to tell		told	
to speak			spoken
to say			

5   Vocabulary – *say, tell,* **etc.**

Complete the spaces with the correct form of
say, tell, speak, or *talk.*

She **told** *me a story about a princess and a*
castle.

1   Does anyone want to .... anything

before the meeting finishes?

2   She can .... three languages.

3   Excuse me, can you .... me the time?

4   OK, the test is just beginning. Stop ....

now and listen to the cassette.

5   I've just .... to Suzy on the phone.

She's got a terrible cold.

6   He .... , 'I'm just going out. Take any

messages for me, please.'

Making a story interesting

1   Adjective order

Put these words in the correct order.

jacket / your / leather / new / brown
your new brown leather jacket

1   shirt / expensive / an / silk
2   car / small / that / Italian
3   young / girls / some / English
4   these / CDs / American / rock
5   computer / my / Power Macintosh / favourite
6   interesting / car / old / an / French

2   Vocabulary – finding the exact word

big large huge **enormous** **gigantic**

small little tiny minute microscopic

unpleasant **bad** *awful* terrible **horrible** *dreadful*

Can you add more words to these? These
words needn't come first in the list.

nice
nervous
unhappy
pretty

3   Another urban legend

Here is another basic urban legend. Refer to
the Student's Book and rewrite the story
adding details.

Many years ago *(when?)* a plane *(what type? what*
nationality?) was flying on a two-hour flight *(from?*
to?) with cargo *(what?)*. There were no passengers
on board the plane, and no flight attendants. At
some point during the flight *(when?)* both the pilot
and the co-pilot fell asleep *(why?)*. The plane was on
auto-pilot. They woke up later. The plane had flown
past its destination *(how far past its destination?)*.
The plane was over a place, a geographical feature
or a country *(what? where?)*. The fuel gauge read
'empty'. Fortunately …*(what happened?)*

This legend began in the 1930s before the auto-pilot was invented. It has been told about planes ever since. Recent versions are sometimes about passenger planes.

Humour

Reflexive pronouns

Complete the spaces with reflexive pronouns – *myself, yourselves*, etc.

1 She bought an instruction manual and taught .... to repair her car.

2 The town .... is pretty boring, but I like the country around it.

3 Why don't we build a new garage .... ? It'll be cheaper than employing a builder.

4 He's got a good sense of humour, and often tells jokes against ....

5 Bill, Anna! Help .... to bread and salad while you're waiting.

6 Jack, be careful! Don't hurt .... !

7 Do you like this sweater? I made it ....

8 They did all the work by .... Nobody helped them.

Telling a funny story

1 The helicopter flight

Every country has images of itself. One British image is that people should keep a 'stiff upper lip'. That is, they shouldn't shout, cry, or make a fuss. This image is strongest in jokes about the British upper classes, and in jokes from the north of England and Scotland. Read the joke, then do the exercises below.

This happened at an agricultural show in Yorkshire. A pilot was selling flights in his helicopter. It was very exciting, because the helicopter didn't have any doors. An old man and an old woman had been watching the flights all day. At five o'clock the pilot said to them, 'Would you like a flight? It's only fifty pounds for fifteen minutes.'

'We'd love to go, we've never been up in a helicopter, but we can't afford that,' said the old woman.

'OK,' said the pilot, 'I've had a pretty good day. If you're very quiet and don't talk, I'll take you up for free.'

The old couple got in, and the pilot decided to show them some stunt flying – some aerobatics. He flew on the side, and then upside down. Finally, he landed. The old man got out.

'Brilliant!' said the pilot, 'You were very quiet. You didn't say a word!'

'It wasn't easy,' said the old man, 'I nearly shouted when my wife fell out.'

2 True or false?

Write *T* (true) or *F* (false).

1 The old couple had never flown in a helicopter before. .....

2 The doors had fallen off the helicopter. .....

3 The old couple had been watching the flights for a couple of hours. .....

4 The pilot had made a lot of money during the day. .....

5 The pilot didn't want them to tell anyone that they weren't paying for the flight. .....

6 The pilot didn't want them to speak during the flight. .....

7 The old man had shouted when his wife fell out. .....

3   Read this joke

It was told by a comedian while he was visiting an old people's home. The audience of elderly people loved it.

> The Queen was visiting an old people's home in Bournemouth. She stopped to speak to one elderly lady.
> 'Do you know who I am?' she said quietly.
> 'No, dear,' replied the old lady, 'I'm afraid I don't. But if you ask that nice nurse over there, I'm sure he'll tell you.'

4   Cultural information

Context is important for many jokes. Here are some points about the context of the joke.
– At the time of the visit, Queen Elizabeth was seventy years old herself.
– Bournemouth has a large population of retired people, and a large number of old people's homes.
– 'Dear' is a very familiar form of address that you would never use to the Queen.
– 'Elderly' is more polite than 'old', and 'lady' is more polite than 'woman'. The polite forms help to give context to the joke.

You could tell the joke about 'a famous person' without saying where it happened, and without 'an old woman' saying 'dear'. Would it be as funny?

5   Questions

What did you think of the joke?

1   How funny was it?
– not funny at all
– mildly amusing
– quite amusing
– very amusing
– hilarious
– hysterical
– the funniest joke you've heard this week

2   Did the joke make you …
– smile?
– laugh quietly to yourself?
– laugh loudly?
– none of the above?

3   Are you going to retell this joke to friends in your own language?

4   Did you think it was …
– stupid?
– unpleasant?
– cruel?
– ageist (offensive to older people)?
– sexist (offensive to women)?
– offensive to people from Bournemouth?
– offensive to people with memory problems?

After you've finished

Skills check

Look at this list of instructions for a minute.

How To Give A Boring Presentation

☆ Don't prepare, just say whatever you can remember at the time.

☆ Don't look at the audience.

☆ Don't worry about sticking to your point. What you say needn't be relevant to the topic of the presentation.

☆ Don't present things in a logical order.

☆ Don't signal what you're going to do next, because you might change your mind or forget what you have signalled.

☆ Speak for a very long time.

☆ Speak in a monotone.

☆ Speak quietly.

☆ People worry too much about tenses, stick to the simple past or simple present, then you won't make so many mistakes.

☆ Don't bother with anecdotes or jokes.

☆ Don't smile – if you do, people will think you're not serious.

☆ If you suddenly think of a joke, tell it. Don't worry about offending anyone.

☆ Don't worry about a conclusion, finish when you're tired.

These instructions are 'wrong'. Do you think that the 'wrong' instructions are easier to remember than the 'right' ones?

If you can't remember things the right way, try writing down opposites. They're often more memorable.

Grammar check

You can test yourself. Choose the correct word.

1 If you (will do / do) regular exercise, you will feel healthier.
2 You should (following / to follow / follow) the instructions carefully.
3 I like listening to music while I (am cooking / was cooking / cooked).
4 Sorry, what did you say? I ('m not / wasn't / didn't) listening.
5 What (were / did / are) you doing at nine o'clock last night?
6 My boss was angry because I (wasn't / hadn't / didn't) finished the project.
7 '(Had / Did / Have) you met them before?' 'No, I hadn't.'
8 He got 30% in the test because he hadn't (finish / finished / finishing) all the questions.
9 In 1992 there (were / had been) 428 nuclear reactors in the world.
10 It was really annoying. I (was having / had / had had) a bath when the phone rang.
11 The driver apologized (when / after / before) the accident.
12 I met two friends while I (had been / was / have been) shopping yesterday.
13 She fell asleep (while / during / when) the film on TV.
14 Deep breathing is (relax / relaxing / relaxed).
15 As soon (when / as / that) you leave the plane, you should go to passport control.
16 A friend of (mine / me / I) called me last night.
17 I was ill last week and I (don't / can't / couldn't) go to work.
18 Comedians often tell jokes about (themselves / they / their) and their families.
19 What (manufacture / made / make) is that car?
20 It's the (funny / funnier / funniest) joke I've ever heard!

UNIT SEVEN

Expressing feelings

Thinking about learning

Classroom activities

I remember an episode, some years ago, when I was in Italy with a group of English friends, and we were driving round one of those seaside towns on the Adriatic coast, looking for a restaurant. Eventually we found a policeman, so we stopped and asked him for directions. The policeman decided that, instead of giving us directions, he would accompany us to the restaurant, so I climbed into the back seat, he got into the passenger seat, and we set off. At the end of the street we came to a set of traffic lights, which were red. Naturally, our driver came to a halt, waiting for the lights to turn green. At this point the policeman turned to the driver, removed his Ray-ban sunglasses and, with obvious bewilderment, asked him what he thought he was doing. By way of explanation, the driver pointed at the red traffic light. The policeman made a series of dismissive gestures, replaced his glasses, and said, 'Nonsense! If everybody behaved like this the traffic would come to a complete standstill. Move on! *Avanti!*'

From *Foreign Bodies* by Peter Collett (Simon & Schuster, 1993)

Imagine that you are the teacher for tomorrow's lesson. You are going to work on the text above. Below are some possible activities for the lesson. You can't do all of them! Which activities would you do? Choose things that you would enjoy and find useful. What sequence would you follow? Make a list. Then compare your list with another student. Are your choices similar or different?

- Read the text silently.
- Ask comprehension questions.
- Listen to a recording with books closed.
- Discuss ideas about minor laws in different countries.
- Explain difficult words.
- Translate the text.
- Repeat some or all of the sentences in the text.
- Listen to a recording and read at the same time.
- Explain grammar.
- Do grammar exercises related to the text.
- Role-play the meeting with the policeman.
- Write out the text.
- Copy examples from the board.
- Practise pronunciation and intonation of some sentences.
- Choose a student to read it aloud.
- Ask true / false questions.
- Students underline difficult words, and compare guesses with partners.
- Refer to dictionaries.
- Dictate some of the text with books closed.
- Do a word network for driving vocabulary on the board.

We are not going to explain anything about the text, because this is not the point of this section.

Feelings

1 Concrete nouns and abstract nouns

You can't see or touch *abstract* nouns. You can see or touch *concrete* nouns. Put these nouns in the appropriate columns.

diploma	wheel	truth	compliment
memory	lips	ability	switch
city	sadness	hair	loneliness
willingness	vegetable	confidence	hope
silicon chip	criticism	house	police officer
time			

concrete nouns	abstract nouns
tree	happiness

2 Word puzzle: abstract nouns

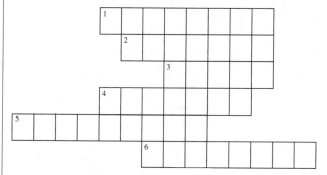

Complete this puzzle with abstract nouns. When you have finished you'll find another noun in one column. What is it?

1 Feeling for other people's problems and worries.
2 You have this feeling when you're not interested in what you are doing.
3 This is a dangerous emotion! It can lead to arguments and even fights.
4 The feeling that you have when you have too many worries and you're feeling nervous.
5 No one likes this when other people are directing it at them.
6 Feeling when you want what someone else has got, or when someone you are interested in prefers someone else.

3 Adjective or adverb?

Choose the correct words.

1 She shouted (angry / angrily).
2 He sounded very (angry / angrily).
3 When he heard the news, his face changed, and he looked (anxious / anxiously).
4 The doctor spoke (sympathetic / sympathetically) to the patient.
5 They seemed (nervous / nervously).
6 I felt (happy / happily) because it was a lovely day.
7 'Are you all right?' he said (kind / kindly).
8 Be careful, that dog seems (aggressive / aggressively).

Compliments

1 Is it a compliment?

Which of these sentences can be used as compliments?

1 Hmm. That's not too bad. .....
2 Hmm. That's not too good. .....
3 I don't think purple's really your colour. .....
4 That really suits you. .....
5 Great tie. .....
6 Yes … I think it's …uh, quite nice. .....
7 That's a very nice name. .....
8 It's not really my style, but it really suits you. .....
9 You look very well. Where have you been? .....
10 It's lovely, but I'm not sure if it suits you. .....
11 Oh, you've changed your hairstyle. .....

2 Responding to compliments

Match the responses with the compliments.

compliments
1 Are those new ear-rings? They match your eyes.
2 Maria Consuela? They're both lovely names.
3 You have three wonderful children.
4 I like your boots.
5 Mm. Great sunglasses.

responses
A Oh, they were very cheap. They're not real gold.
B Thank you. Blue's my favourite colour.
C They're very old. I've had them for years.
D Thank you. I think so too.
E Thank you. They're Spanish. My grandparents came from Mexico.

3 Giving compliments

Choose compliments for these situations.

1 A colleague has just returned from a holiday. Your colleague looks happy and relaxed and very healthy.
2 Your boss has just arrived at work with a new hairstyle. Actually, you don't think the hairstyle suits your boss.
3 Someone has just introduced you to a person with an unusual and interesting name.

4 A colleague is wearing a new perfume or aftershave.

5 You've just finished dinner at a friend's house. It was an excellent meal. Your friend cooked it.

6 A relative has been on a diet and lost weight. The relative looks much thinner.

7 Your friend is wearing a new suit. It's obviously expensive and your friend is very proud of it.

Thanks

1 Matching

When would you say these things? Match the thanks with the situations.

thanks
1 That's OK. Thanks for looking.
2 Thank you. I appreciate your help very much.
3 Thanks for the ride.
4 Thanks for having me.
5 Thanks for inviting me. I enjoyed myself very much.
6 And thanks for the meal. It was wonderful.
7 Thanking you in anticipation.
8 Thanks. It's just what I wanted.

situations
A The end of a formal business letter where you have requested something from the person receiving the letter.
B Receiving a birthday present.
C Saying goodbye to a business acquaintance, after a visit to a foreign country.
D After a party.
E Getting out of someone else's car.
F A record shop. The assistant has tried unsuccessfully to find a CD for you.
G Leaving a restaurant after someone else has paid the bill.
H At the end of a stay at a friend's home.

2 Responding to thanks

Write responses to the thanks. Complete the spaces. Write different responses for each situation.

1 You're holding the door open for a stranger in a shop. The stranger is a young woman.
STRANGER: Thanks.

YOU: ....

2 Your boss has lost a pen. You've just found it.
BOSS: Thank you very much.

YOU: ....

3 You found a wallet with some credit cards in it. You've taken it to the owner's house.
OWNER: Thank you! You've been very kind. I hope you didn't go to too much trouble.

YOU: ....

4 You've taken a business acquaintance to lunch, and you've paid the bill. You enjoyed the meal and conversation.
ACQUAINTANCE: That was a lovely meal. Thank you.

YOU: ....

Praise and appreciation

1 Assessment

Look at this employee assessment form. Shelley Lee works for the All Seasons Hotel Group. She's a trainee manager.

ALL SEASONS HOTEL GROUP

Employee assessment, February

Last name:	Lee
First name:	Shelley
Middle initial:	E
Workplace:	All Seasons Plaza Hotel, Ottawa, Canada
Timekeeping:	Shelley has always been at work on time.
Helpfulness:	Shelley has been very helpful to guests.
Politeness:	Shelley is usually polite and courteous, but she should be careful with difficult guests. She has sometimes answered them rudely.
Working by yourself:	Shelley has not needed to ask questions about the job. She has worked well without supervision.
Willingness:	Shelley has volunteered for extra work, and has never complained about extra hours.
Test scores:	Shelley got a low score on her first test, but has improved slightly in recent tests. She doesn't study enough for tests.
General:	Shelley is an excellent employee who has done well in her first three months with us. We wish her every success for the future.

Answer the questions.

1 Which tense is used most for assessing Shelley's work? Is it the present simple, the present perfect simple, or the past simple tense?
2 Look at the comments about Shelley. How many praise her? How many criticize her?

2 Showing appreciation

Here are some sentences about appreciation. Choose the correct words.

1 If someone parked my car at a hotel (I'd / I'll) tip them.
2 I (won't / wouldn't) tip the waiter if the service were bad.
3 If the hairdressing salon owner (did / does) my hair, I wouldn't give them a tip.
4 If a business acquaintance gave me an expensive present, (I'll / I'd) be embarrassed.
5 I (wouldn't / don't) clap if a concert were bad.
6 If I went to dinner with a business acquaintance, I (would / will) take some flowers.

3 Type 2 conditionals

Change these type 1 conditional sentences into type 2 conditional sentences.

I'll do it if I can.
I'd do it if I could.

1 If I'm in London, I'll visit the Houses of Parliament.
2 The waiter will be happy if I leave a big tip.
3 If my boss compliments me, I'll thank her.
4 If I don't understand, I'll ask the teacher to repeat more slowly.
5 I'll be late if I miss the train.
6 I won't go out if it rains.

Criticism

1 Reactions to criticism

Imagine you are working on a job with other people. A supervisor comes over and says, 'Oh, no! You're all doing it wrong!'

This is how the people with you react.

A: It's not my fault! I've had a lot of personal problems recently.
B: Don't blame us! No one gave us any instructions.
C: OK. Do you think you can do it better?
D: Sorry. We'll try again.
E: Sorry. Can you explain the problem?

Which of the reactions are negative and which are positive? Who would you rather work with – A, B, C, D, or E?

2 Dealing with criticism

HOW TO BE
successful
IN LIFE
Dr. Lauren K. Beckenbauer *42*

Chapter 9: Criticism
Many people find it difficult to accept criticism.

The supervisor
When you have to criticize someone, follow these steps:

- Before you criticize, say something positive. Give a compliment, show appreciation of work that has been done.
- Show that you understand the difficulties.
- Don't be personal – criticize the action, not the person.
- State the problem clearly.
- Offer a solution to further problems.
- Don't give threats or warnings.
- Ask what you can do to help.
- Let the person ask you questions.
- Give compliments when the fault is corrected.

The employee
When you have to accept criticism, try to do these things:

- Listen without interrupting.
- Don't be defensive. Accept it when you are wrong.
- Don't give excuses which aren't relevant.
- Apologize and promise to correct the problem.
- Make sure you understand what's wrong. Ask people to repeat explanations if you don't understand.
- Don't be afraid to ask for help.

Look at this dialogue. Which sentences would Dr Beckenbauer approve of? (✔) Which ones would she disapprove of? (✘)

..... SUPERVISOR: Good morning, Josh. You look very smart today. Is that a new suit?

..... EMPLOYEE: Yes, it is.

..... SUPERVISOR: I've just been on the phone with Mr Barratt. He's a difficult customer, isn't he?

..... EMPLOYEE: Did he complain about me? Well, it was all his fault.

..... SUPERVISOR: He didn't complain exactly. But he told me that you had an argument with him. He said you were pretty angry.

..... EMPLOYEE: Well, he's a complete idiot. He started the argument.

..... SUPERVISOR: He is a customer, Josh. You know what they say, 'the customer is always right.'

..... EMPLOYEE: Not this time.

..... SUPERVISOR: Well, next time he calls, maybe I should speak to him. We don't want to lose his business.

..... EMPLOYEE: I don't understand. What do you mean?

..... SUPERVISOR: You get angry much too quickly, Josh. You have a bad temper. If it happens again, I'll have to speak to the Managing Director.

..... EMPLOYEE: Is that a threat? Why are you telling me about it … ?

..... SUPERVISOR: I don't have time for this. Just put his calls through to me, OK?

Being a good listener

1 *for* and *since*

You use *for* with periods of time (e.g. *for ten years*) and *since* with points in time (e.g. *since 1996*). Complete the spaces with *for* or *since*.

1	.... Thursday	6	.... ten minutes
2	.... two hours	7	.... February 29th
3	.... a long time	8	.... three days
4	.... 7.30	9	.... several years
5	.... I came here	10	.... last week

2 Present perfect continuous

Write full answers to these questions.

1 How long have you been studying English?
2 How long have you been living in your present home?
3 How long have you been using *Handshake*?
4 How long have you been working in your present job / attending your present school?

3 Reflective listening

Complete the spaces in this conversation. The speaker is very upset. Don't give advice or opinions. Don't ask direct questions. Use reflective listening techniques. You can look at the Student's Book, exercise 3, and the Listening transcript.

SPEAKER: That's it! I've had enough of this job!

YOU: ....

SPEAKER: Angry? I'm absolutely furious! I'm leaving, I can't stay here any more.

YOU: ....

SPEAKER: It's Mr Jones, the new Sales Director. He asked me … no, he told me … to empty his wastebin.

YOU: ....

SPEAKER: I'm a qualified translator. I can speak three languages! I'm not the office cleaner.

YOU: ....

SPEAKER: I'm going to empty his wastebin onto his desk! That's what I'm going to do!

YOU: ....

SPEAKER: Not really. Maybe I should just tell him that's it's not my job. Oh, thanks for listening. You've been a great help.

How often do you get angry?

1 Find the different sound

All these words are from unit seven. Put a ring around the word in each line which has a different underlined vowel sound.

m<u>a</u>d	w<u>a</u>ste	br<u>ea</u>k	pr<u>ai</u>se
q<u>ueu</u>e	h<u>u</u>mour	b<u>u</u>lb	f<u>u</u>rious
l<u>ea</u>st	pl<u>ea</u>sed	m<u>e</u>nial	sw<u>ea</u>ty
t<u>i</u>p	k<u>i</u>nd	l<u>i</u>pstick	f<u>i</u>gure
j<u>ea</u>lous	regr<u>e</u>t	gr<u>ea</u>t	r<u>e</u>ject
<u>o</u>wner	pr<u>o</u>blem	ap<u>o</u>logize	<u>o</u>ffice
dr<u>i</u>ve	l<u>i</u>ght	critic<u>i</u>ze	<u>i</u>nferior

2 Grading words

Grade these frequency adverbs from least often to most often.

normally	rarely	sometimes	hardly ever
always	never	nearly always	

Grade these verbs from like most to like least.

dislike	love	like	hate	don't mind

Grade these time words from most recent to least recent.

an hour ago	yesterday	five minutes ago
last week	in 1995	a fortnight ago
in June		

3 Matching

Match the verbs in the first column with nouns in the second column. All these examples are in unit seven.

solve	your temper
build	on something
give	your appreciation
show	a problem
lose	an instruction
comment	a friendship

Complaining

1 Aggressive body language

What are these people doing? Label the pictures.

1 waving arms
2 pushing the chin forward
3 hands on hips
4 pointing finger
5 folding arms
6 standing with feet apart

2 Aggressive, submissive, or assertive?

Put the words in the appropriate places on the table.

actions:	speaking calmly, shouting, whining
attitude:	hesitant and nervous, reasonable, unreasonable
eyes:	good eye contact, looking down, staring
speech:	clear and direct, loud, quiet
words used:	*You'd better …, Why don't we …, I wonder if you could …*

aggressive behaviour	submissive behaviour	assertive behaviour

3 Vocabulary

Complete the spaces with these words.

return	receipt	repair	refund

1 Good morning. I want a .... for this suitcase. It's no good at all, and it cost £120 yesterday. I'd like my money back.

2 Have you got a .... ? We can't give you your money back if you haven't got one.

3 Hello. I'd like to .... this sweater. It's not my size.

4 So the radio isn't working. Bring it back to the shop. I'm sure we can .... it.

4 Verbs and nouns

Complete the table.

verb	noun
apologize	apology
....	complaint
behave	....
....	suggestion
criticize	....

5 Making a complaint

How would you complain in these situations? Write what you would say.

1 You've been waiting in a queue for five minutes in a shop. A person has just walked in front of you, and the assistant has started to serve the person.

2 You've just arrived at a garage to collect your car after a 10,000 km service. There's oil on the seat, and the car smells of petrol.

3 You phoned a company. The operator asked you to wait, and you had to listen to a very loud tape of an opera singer for three minutes. You've just got through to the person you wanted.

Dealing with complaints

1 Customer comments

Many restaurants and hotels have 'comments books' where customers can give their opinion of the service. This is from the comments book at the Little Cook restaurant on the M3 motorway in Britain.

Little Cook Restaurants plc	
Customer comments	
Restaurant: Dodge Lee Services, M3	
Week beginning: March 4th	
day time comment name	Monday 7.15 I waited a long time, and when my breakfast arrived the eggs were completely cold. MP White, London
day time comment name	Monday 7.50 A lovely meal! We all enjoyed it. Pleasant, friendly service. We'll stop at the Little Cook again! Mr & Mrs D Smith, Bournemouth
day time comment name	Monday 8.45 Service was slow. I was in a hurry, and I waited 15 minutes for a coffee and doughnut. Mrs E David, Poole
day time comment name	monday 10.30 I think £2.80 for a weak tea and a Danish pastry is much too expensive. Then the waiter expected a tip! R Carrier, Southampton
day time comment name	Monday 12.15 There was only one vegetarian meal on the menu, and it was terrible! You should have more vegetarian food. Ms L McCartney, Hounslow
day time comment name	monday 12.45 Very nice. Thank you. Mr & Mrs H Johnson, Exeter
day time comment name	monday 1.50 The table was dirty, the ashtrays were full, and there were no seats in the no-smoking section. My clothes smell of smoke now. Ms J Player, Bristol
day time comment name	Monday 2.25 I sat down and the seat was covered with chocolate milk shake! My best suit is completely ruined, and I have an important meeting this afternoon. Mr R Blanc, Oxford

M P White ate the cold eggs. Would you have eaten the eggs?
I would have eaten the eggs. or
I wouldn't have eaten the eggs. or
I would have asked for more eggs.

Answer in the same way. You decide on the answer.

1 Mrs Smith thought the meal was OK, not great, but she liked the waiter. In the same situation, would you have written something nice in the comments book?
2 Mrs David waited a long time. Would you have waited that long?
3 Mr Carrier paid with three pound coins and waited for his 20p change. Would you have waited for the change?
4 Ms McCartney is a vegetarian and worries about the quality of her food. In her situation, would you have stopped for lunch at a motorway services?
5 Mr and Mrs Johnson didn't enjoy their meal, but like many English people they never complain. Imagine that you had been in the same situation. Would you have written a positive comment in the book, or just written nothing?
6 Ms Player was a non-smoker, but she sat in the smoking section. Imagine that you were her. Would you have sat in the smoking section?
7 Mr Blanc didn't look at the seat before he sat down. Would you have looked at the seat first?
8 If this had happened to you, would you have asked for money for dry-cleaning?

2 What would you have done?

I left the dinner in the cooker for too long and it was burned! I didn't know whether to eat it or throw it away.
I would have eaten it.

1 My boss offered me more money or longer holidays. I didn't know whether to take the money or the holidays.
2 I bought some new socks, but they were the wrong size. They were very cheap. I didn't know whether to take them back to the shop or not.

3 Last year, I won a choice of two holidays in a competition. I didn't know whether to go to Florida or to London.

3 Reading – culture comparison

Read this text. Every tenth word is missing. Can you complete the spaces?

British people are famous for not complaining even when .... food and service are terrible. They just say quietly, ' .... nice, thank you very much.' People who work in .... say that the Americans complain more than the British, ... that the Japanese complain less than either. The Swiss .... famous for complaining, and are proud of their reputation. .... few years ago the national airline, Swissair, made a .... series of adverts which joked about the Swiss habit .... complaining about bad service. The idea of the adverts .... that an airline which could satisfy the Swiss, could .... anybody in the world.

Would you be more likely to complain in your own country than in a foreign country? Explain why / why not.

Difficult questions

1 Sticking to the point

Rewrite these sentences in the correct order.

point. / Please / the / to / stick
Please stick to the point.

1 haven't / question / my / You / answered / yet.
2 back / get / Let's / the / to / point.
3 question? / you / answer / my / Could
4 still / had / answer. / I / an / haven't
5 subject. / are / changing / You / the
6 question. / to / an / I / answer /want / my / original
7 issue. / think / avoiding / you're / I / the
8 reply / I / had / yet. / a / haven't

2 Avoiding the issue

The sentences below are from an interview.
In each of them, the speaker is avoiding the
issue. Match the sentences to the techniques.

sentence

1 I'm pleased that you asked me that.
2 This question reminds me of a story.
3 I'm afraid this is a private matter, and it's none
   of your business.
4 There are good arguments both for and
   against this question.
5 Could you repeat the question? I'm afraid I
   didn't quite get your point.

technique

A changing the subject
B 'sitting on the fence' – trying to be neutral or
   non-committal
C commenting on the question without replying
D giving yourself more time to think
E directly refusing to answer

After you've finished

Skills check

**Should you feel good about yourself, or
should you feel guilty?**

Answer truthfully about the last 24 hours.
Tick the boxes.

Nice behaviour
☐ Have you thanked someone for
   doing something?
☐ Have you congratulated someone?
☐ Have you complimented someone?
☐ Have you praised someone's work?
☐ Have you offered to help someone?
☐ Have you been a sympathetic listener?

Nasty behaviour
☐ Have you blamed someone for
   doing something?
☐ Have you criticized someone?
☐ Have you insulted someone?
☐ Have you complained about
   something?
☐ Have you refused to help someone?
☐ Have you lost your temper with
   someone?

Grammar check

You can test yourself. Choose the correct
word.

1   I think political programmes on TV are
    (bored / boring / boredom).
2   She doesn't like (critical / criticism /
    criticize) of her work.
3   His aftershave smells (good / nicely /
    well).
4   'Thank you very much.' 'That's OK, don't
    (matter / mind / mention) it.'
5   He has been working on this project (by /
    since / for) two years.
6   How long have you been (living / lived /
    live) in your present home?
7   If I (would be / were / was) you, I'd get a
    mobile phone.
8   I get annoyed (while / when / why) no-
    one answers the phone.
9   If I won a lot of money, I ('d / 'll / 'm)
    buy a new house.
10 You'd (must / should / better) be careful!
11 It's late. I ought (go / going / to go) soon.
12 I'm afraid your room won't be ready
    (unless / until / since) midday.
13 Excuse me, I ('d like / 'll like / like) to see
    the manager.
14 If I'd got up earlier, I (didn't / won't /
    wouldn't) have missed my train.
15 I would (had / have) called if I'd had
    time.
16 Don't let them (interrupt / to interrupt /
    interrupting).
17 Never waste time (for blaming / blaming /
    to blame) other people.
18 What would you have done? (Had / Did /
    Would) you have put the phone down?
19 I get impatient when I (have / must /
    got) to stand in line.
20 He rarely loses his (annoying / angry /
    temper).

Thinking about learning

Your future

1 How are you going to use your English in the future?

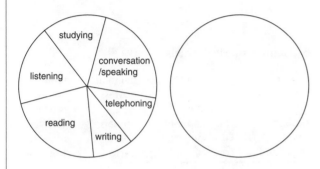

Look at the pie chart on the left. Make up a chart for yourself in the other circle.
If you're going to read in English, what are you going to read?
☐ reference books   ☐ documents
☐ instructions   ☐ newspapers
☐ literature   ☐ magazines

What are you going to write?
☐ faxes   ☐ e-mail
☐ letters   ☐ lecture notes
☐ reports   ☐ forms

Where are you going to use English?
☐ in my country
☐ in English-speaking countries
☐ in other countries
☐ for international communication

2 Are you going to continue your studies in English?

After you've finished this course, are you going to study another course?
☐ Yes   ☐ No   ☐ Don't know

If you've answered 'Yes', will this course be:
☐ general English?
☐ English for specific purposes?
☐ an examination course?

If you're going to study English for specific purposes, which of the following areas are you going to study?
☐ general business   ☐ marketing
☐ technical   ☐ tourism
☐ hotel and catering ☐ medical
☐ science   ☐ engineering
☐ air transport   ☐ academic purposes
☐ other ....

3 How are you going to keep up your English?

Which of the following ways might you use to keep up your English?
☐ self-study
☐ listening to radio (e.g. BBC World Service)
☐ watching TV programmes
☐ watching movies / videos
☐ reading newspapers and magazines
☐ reading simplified readers
☐ writing to a pen friend
☐ listening to rock music
☐ travelling to English-speaking countries
☐ joining a conversation club
☐ in my community

Rumour and gossip

1 *want someone to do something*

Write sentences as in the example.

Some men are arriving with a vending machine.
*Where do you want **them** to put **it**?*

1 Sara's coming soon with the photocopies.
2 The TV repair man's going to bring the TV this afternoon.
3 They'll deliver the new desk later.
4 I'm bringing the reports to your office.
5 We're going to carry the photocopier into the reception area.

2 *sorry to hear ...*

Complete the spaces with these words.

sorry	pleased	surprised	disgusted	sad

1 I was really .... to see that London Zoo's giant panda had died.

2 I'm .... to hear that Anna has failed her exams.

3 Congratulations! I was really .... to hear your good news.

4 I was .... to see him at the party. I thought he was in hospital.

5 I was .... to find a hair in my salad.

Looking for the truth

1 Matching

Match the sentences which mean the same.

1 It's true.
2 I don't know whether it's true or not.
3 I don't think it's true, but I'm not certain.
4 It's not true.

A It might be true.
B It could be true.
C It can't be true.
D It must be true.

2 *It could be mine ...*

Complete the spaces with *must be ...*, *can't be ...*, or *could be ...*

A: Is it yours?
B: Let me see. *It could be mine.* I'm not sure.

1 A: Is the suitcase hers?
  B: .... It's got her name on it.

2 A: Are the figures correct?
  B: .... The numbers in the last column don't add up.

3 A: Is Brad Canadian?
  B: I'm not sure. .... His accent is either Canadian or American.

4 A: Are they hungry?
  B: .... They haven't eaten all day.

5 A: Is that the new Bruce Springsteen CD they're playing?
  B: I don't know. .... It sounds quite like him.

6 A: Is that watch real gold?
  B: .... It only costs thirty dollars.

3 Gender-marked words

brother	president	bellman	aunt
farmer	office junior	hostess	landlady
author	grandparent	wife	assistant
husband	chambermaid	human	waiter
bride	Englishman	operator	princess
boyfriend	cowboy	person	shopgirl

Put these words into three groups on the table below.

must be male, can't be female	must be female, can't be male	could be male or female

Underline the gender-marked words which can be replaced by inclusive words.

Facts, deduction, speculation

1 Matching

Match the sentences which mean the same.

1 It happened. There's no question about it.
2 It certainly didn't happen. That's impossible.
3 I don't know whether it happened or not.
4 I don't think that it happened, but there is a small possibility.

A It could have happened.
B It must have happened.
C It might have happened.
D It can't have happened.

2 The past of modals

Perhaps they went home early. (might)
They might have gone home early.

Rewrite these sentences in the same way.

1 She didn't know him. It's impossible. (can't)
2 I'm sure you met him. (must)
3 It's possible that I've left it in the office. (might)
4 Maybe she hasn't heard the news. (might not)
5 Perhaps he forgot the meeting. (could)
6 I'm sure we've missed the flight. (must)
7 Maybe they were at home. (might)
8 He didn't do it. (can't)

3 Past perfect continuous

Last night, Jim came home at 8 p.m. He was very tired.
(he / work hard / all day)
He had been working hard all day.

Make sentences in the same way.

1 When she woke up, she felt really frightened, and for a few seconds she thought she was somewhere else.
(she / have / bad dream)
2 When she walked into her daughter's room she could smell cigarette smoke. Her daughter was with a friend.
(they / smoke)
3 Sorry I was rude when you phoned last night. It was 8.45.
(I / watch / my favourite TV programme)
4 When we came out of the cinema the sun was shining, but there was water on the road and pavement.
(it / rain)
5 When I finally got through to the complaints department on the phone, I was feeling really angry.
(I / wait / for ten minutes)

4 You must have been feeling angry!

I had been holding the phone for ten minutes, and I had to listen to this loud music the whole time! (must)
You must have been feeling angry. / You must have been angry.

React to these situations in the same way.

1 We'd been walking in the snow for two hours, and the temperature was minus five degrees Celsius! (must)
2 Mike was very quiet this morning. He's usually so friendly and cheerful. Then he went home early. I wonder if he was feeling well? (can't)
3 The team had been playing for ninety minutes in the hot sun. The score was 1-1, and they then had to play thirty minutes extra time. (must)

Changing times

1 Why?

Look back at exercise 3 in **Facts, deduction, speculation** above. Look at the example sentence.

Why was he tired?
He was tired because he had been working hard all day.

Answer about the other sentences in the exercise, writing sentences with *because.*

1 Why was she frightened when she woke up?
2 Why was the girl's mother angry?
3 Why was the speaker rude?
4 Why was there water on the pavement?
5 Why was the speaker feeling angry?

2 *because / because of*

Underline the correct words in brackets.

1 We didn't enjoy our holiday because of (the terrible weather / the weather was terrible).
2 I'd been saving money because (a new car / I wanted a new car).

3 They must have been worried because (the news was bad / bad news).

4 I stayed at home because of (I had a cold / my cold).

5 They moved to Bristol because of (she had a new job / her new job).

6 Because (your mistake / you made a mistake), we lost a lot of business.

3 Employment

Check the meaning of these words and then complete the spaces.

strike	redundant	leisure
losses	unemployment	created

1 People are worried because of rising

....

2 My uncle was made .... after thirty years in the same job.

3 Last year there were 40,000 job .... in manufacturing because of automation.

4 The computer industry has .... many new jobs.

5 Air traffic controllers are going on .... because they want more money.

6 Because people have more .... time, there are more jobs in the entertainment industry.

4 Jobs

Which people might work for these employers? List them on the chart.

THIS WEEK
The weekly news and entertainment magazine
134 Farringdon Street • London • EC2 4ER

THE NATIONAL MIDLAND BANK PLC

Head Office: NatMid Tower, Canary Wharf, London

The Grange Hospital

Gormley Park, Winchester, Hampshire SO23 4RT

journalists	doctors	designers
nurses	photographers	secretaries
editors	security officers	bank clerks
receptionists	computer operators	telephonists
managers	lawyers	messengers
cleaners	artists	data processors
pharmacists	accountants	porters
supervisors	cooks	

This Week magazine	National Midland Bank	The Grange Hospital

5 Spelling

Make three lists. You can use words from exercise 4, and you can add any others that you know.

1 Jobs ending in -er (e.g. engineer).
2 Jobs ending in -or (e.g. author).
3 Jobs ending in -ist (e.g. dentist).

Understanding each other

1 Vocabulary: losing a job

There are several ways of telling someone that they have *lost their job* and that they're *unemployed* or *out of work*.

Newspapers have headlines like *200 JOBS AXED AT CAR FACTORY*.

'You're *sacked*' (mainly UK) and 'You're *fired*' are very aggressive ways of *dismissing* someone. We usually prefer to tell people indirectly. In Britain they say 'people have been *made redundant*' and in America 'people have been *let go*'.

'We're going to have to *let you go*' suggests that the employee wants to be *allowed to leave* the company, and that the company is reluctantly accepting their request. The idea is that the employee has *resigned* (UK) or *quit* (USA), when really they've been fired.

Read the text. Are these sentences true or false?

1 'You're sacked' is a pleasant way of telling someone that they're redundant. .....
2 'We'll have to let you go' is more common in American English. .....
3 When you decide to leave a job for your own reasons, you're fired. .....
4 When someone does something wrong, the employer might dismiss them. .....
5 When someone finds a better job with another company, they resign or quit from their old job. .....
6 When business gets better, companies have to let employees go. .....
7 You can quit a computer program (but you cannot resign from it!). .....

2 Body language

Match the sentences with the body language.

1 'Now, you listen to me ...'
2 'I think we agree ...'
3 'I don't care what you say. I don't agree.'
4 'But it's not my fault ...'

A showing the palms of your hands
B folding your arms
C pointing your finger
D mirroring each other

Paraphrasing

1 Link words – *and, but, because*

Choose the best words to complete the spaces.

1 I'm going to the bank .... I need some money.
2 I'm going to the supermarket .... I'm not going to buy anything. I'm meeting a friend there.
3 It's going to rain tomorrow .... it's going to be very cold, too.
4 I've met her, ... I haven't met her sister.
5 They're good at algebra .... they're good at chemistry, too.

2 Guess the meaning (1)

Match the idiomatic sentences (1–5) with the listener's paraphrases (A–E). You'll have to guess some of them.

1 Sorry, I haven't got a clue!
2 No offence. I was just having a laugh.
3 Come on! You must think I was born yesterday!
4 Don't look at me! I had nothing to do with it.
5 I'm absolutely boiling mad!

A You mean it wasn't your fault.
B You mean you're angry.
C You mean you don't know the answer.
D You mean you were joking.
E You mean you don't believe me.

3 Guess the meaning (2)

This is more difficult. Look at the idiomatic expressions below. Paraphrase them as in exercise 2. Use these adjectives.

bored	hungry	annoying	thirsty	excited
cheap	cold	expensive	happy	

After they'd won the match, the team were completely over the moon!
You mean they were happy.

1 No, thanks! I'm full up. I couldn't eat another thing!

2   That new car cost an arm and a leg!

3   I'm going to buy that shirt. It costs peanuts.

4   What a film! I couldn't keep my eyes open.

5   What a film! I was on the edge of my seat!

6   Thanks, I needed that. I was really dry.

7   Stop singing, it really gets on my nerves.

8   It's freezing! You could freeze to death out here.

The answers you want

1   Comments

Daniel Elgin asked everyone to complete the survey in the Student's Book. Then he also invited them to add any comments they wanted to. Daniel only wrote down the comments he agreed with. Which ones did he write down? Tick them.

1   'I don't drink tea or coffee because they're bad for your health.'
Mr Nibbs, Accounts   .....

2   'Tea from vending machines tastes like washing-up water.'
Ms Singh, Data Processing   .....

3   'My coffee was cold this morning because it had been on the trolley for half an hour.'
Mr Partridge, Sales   .....

4   'I can't understand this questionnaire.'
Mrs Grove, Publicity   .....

5   'Will the machines sell soup? I like hot soup.'
Mr Parsons, Factory   .....

6   'How much will the drinks cost from the machines?'
Miss Harris, Mail room   .....

7   'I have tried coffee from vending machines before, and it's excellent.'
Mr Marriot, Managing Director   .....

8   'It's obvious. The company just wants to save money.'
Ms Scargill, Marketing   .....

9   'Tea breaks are a waste of time. I prefer to get on with my work. I can drink tea while I'm working.'
Mr Crawley, Supervisor   .....

10   'I can't answer this now because it's my tea-break. Come back later.'
Ms Macintosh, Computing   .....

11   'Tea ladies are very important, and they work very hard for very little money!'
Mrs Twining, Tea lady   .....

2   Find the different sound

All these words are from unit eight. Put a ring around the word in each line which has a different underlined vowel sound.

taste	natural	waste	faint
farmer	palm	machine	partner
routine	union	rumour	point
starting	heart	heard	marked
nurse	worker	personnel	security
risen	miner	division	cash till
created	restaurant	vending	messenger

3   Compound nouns

Compound nouns have two (or more) words. Match the words from the first column with words from the second column. All the words are from unit eight.

national	machine
vending	director
trade	union
tea	resources
managing	processor
natural	insurance
systems	trolley
data	consultant

Consequences

1   Definition

consequence /ˈkɒnsɪkwəns; US -kwens/ noun 1 [C] something that follows as a result or effect of sth else: *The power station was shown to be dangerous and, as a consequence, was closed down.* o *The error had tragic consequences.* 2 [U] (formal) importance: *It is of no consequence.*
consequent /ˈkɒnsɪkwənt/ adj (formal) following as the result of sth else: *The lack of rain and consequent poor harvests have led to food shortages.*
consequently adv: *She didn't work hard enough, and consequently failed the exam.*

From the *Oxford Wordpower Dictionary*

Read the dictionary definition and find abbreviations for:

1 countable
2 uncountable
3 something
4 adjective
5 adverb
6 American pronunciation.

2 Consequences

Read the definition and complete the spaces in the sentences with these words.

consequently	as	consequence	consequent

1 They don't matter. They're of no ....

2 She lost her driving licence after the accident, and .... a consequence she lost her job.

3 The hot summer and .... low rainfall caused water shortages in the West of England.

4 He got good grades in his exams, and .... got a better job.

3 Changes

Penbevan, Cornwall

Penbevan is a pleasant quiet fishing village, about ten miles from Penzance in Cornwall. Population 709. Early closing day: Wednesday. Two small hotels. One restaurant.

The Fisherman's Friend. 12 rooms, 6 en-suite bathroom. No pets. Licensed bar. Restaurant. Parking.

The Red Lion. 9 rooms. 3 with shower / WC. Pub accommodation. No parking. No pets.

The Beachside Café. Seats 45. Licensed. Lunch and dinner. No reservations needed. Closed: Thursdays, Sundays. MasterCard. Visa.

The Atlantic Club Hotel Group wants to build a 2000-bed holiday resort just outside Penbevan. It would employ 350 people. Some of the local people are for the plan, while others are against it. But what would the consequences of the new resort be? Complete the spaces.

1 If they built the hotel, there .... be more jobs.

2 The village is small. A lot of workers would come from other places. Consequently there .... be more traffic in the area.

3 If there .... more traffic, they would have to improve the roads.

4 If they .... the roads, more people would visit the village.

5 If more people visited the village, it .... be quiet anymore.

6 If it weren't quiet, some people .... move from the village.

7 If more people came, local businesses .... make more money.

8 ....
....

Can you add another sentence about the consequences?

4 How would you feel?

If you lived in Penbevan, how would you feel? Imagine that you are the people below. Complete the sentences.

1 A young unemployed person, aged 18
'If they built the resort …

2 A fisherman.
'If there were more people, there'd be more boats. If there were more boats …'

3 A retired person, aged 75.
'If the village became busier …'

4 The owner of The Red Lion.
'If people were staying at the new resort …'

83

5 A parent with two young children.
'If there were more traffic …'
6 A farmer, whose farm they want to buy for the resort. They've offered £3 million.
'If they bought my farm …'
7 The new manager of the resort who lives in London at the moment.
'If I moved to Penbevan …'

8 ....

....

Can you think of another sentence for number 8?

Reason and result

1 Another report from Daniel

Daniel Elgin has written a report on waste-bins. Read it. Complete the spaces with these words.

so that	to sum up	therefore
as a result	because of	

Office waste-bins

We have a large number of metal waste-bins in the offices. The cleaners empty them every evening. The bins are often dirty, and .... this, the cleaners sometimes have to wash them, and .... they soon become rusty. ...., after about three years we need to buy new ones. These cost £50 each, and we replace around thirty every year. If we used plastic bags (bin liners), the bins would stay clean. The cleaners could empty them more quickly, ... we would need fewer cleaners ...., I believe that we should begin using bin liners as soon as possible.

2 Sharon's argument

Sharon Maxwell didn't agree with Daniel. Read her argument. Every tenth word is missing. Can you complete the spaces?

Office waste-bins

95% of the waste in the bins is paper. .... there were bin liners, people would throw more things .... them; half-empty yoghurt pots, half-empty soft drink cans, fruit .... so on. At present they take these things to .... kitchen. The liners often have small holes in them, ... yoghurt and liquid would leak through the holes. As .... result there would be bad smells in the office. .... we used liners, the cleaners wouldn't wash the bins .... Also, they'd carry away the rubbish in the bin .... instead of carrying the waste bins. Yoghurt and liquid .... fall onto the carpets and .... floors. Therefore, if we .... bin liners, the office would be dirtier. Also, you .... throw away or burn paper. Burning plastic is bad .... the environment. Finally, the liners cost 8p each and .... employee would need five every week. Therefore it would .... more than £20 a year for each employee. My .... is that we should continue with the present system.

3 Checking comprehension

If you did the exercises successfully, you must have understood enough of the arguments! However, look through the two reports and find words with these meanings.

1 A British English word. The Americans prefer 'trash'.
2 The name for a plastic bag that you put inside bins.

3 A word that means the same as half-full.
4 A general word for things like water, cola, milk, fruit juice, disinfectant.
5 When iron and steel are wet for a long time, they go red. The adjective which means this.
6 They're made of wool or nylon and you put them on the floor inside a building.
7 A verb which you use when liquid comes through a container accidentally.

4 Who do you agree with?

Write a sentence which begins:
I agree with (Sharon / Daniel) because …

Expressing opinions

Opinions

Bin liners were discussed at a meeting. These were some of the opinions.

> **Sharon Maxwell, PA to the Managing Director**
> 'I strongly disagree with Mr Elgin's idea. I don't think we should start using bin liners for all the the reasons I have given in my report, which you have seen.'

> **Roz Hardie, Trade union**
> 'The most important point here is job losses. How many cleaners do you intend to make redundant? I can't agree with the proposal. This is against our agreement about job losses in the contract of the 17th of November 1995, section 2, paragraph 3.'

> **Daniel Elgin, Systems consultant**
> '67.3% of companies use bin liners, and I estimate a saving of £7.28 per employee over 156 weeks, plus a saving of two cleaners' wages per week.'

> **Florence Mayfield, Cleaner**
> 'I do my best and I can't do any more. I've been here for ten years and nobody's complained about my work. I keep the waste bins very clean.'

> **Alistair Marriot, Managing Director**
> 'You've all made very good arguments, and I'd like to thank you for your points of view. There are advantages and disadvantages to all new ideas, and I will be considering the possibilities.'

During the discussion, people took different positions. Which people argued in these ways?

1 emotional argument
2 factual and statistical argument
3 legal argument
4 'sitting on the fence' – the chairperson's role
5 criticizing

After you've finished

Skills check

Checklist for discussions

You are having a discussion. Can you assess your abilities in English? Write *C* – confident, or *?* – need more practice.

..... Can you explain your point of view?
..... Can you use body language to emphasize your points?
..... Can you give reasons to explain your opinions?
..... Can you explain the consequences of your ideas?
..... Can you agree with people's opinions?
..... Can you disagree with people's opinions?
..... Can you use paraphrasing to check information?
..... Can you use paraphrasing to explain your ideas in a different way?
..... Can you sum up the main points of a discussion?

Grammar check

You can test yourself. Choose the correct word.

1 They're going to (installation / installing / install) new machines.
2 I'm not sure what happened. She may

(has / had / have) fainted.

3 I don't know who he is. He could (to be / being / be) the manager.

4 She had (heard / hear / hearing) her talking on the phone.

5 That must have (was / be / been) expensive.

6 People have more free time nowadays (because of / because / so) machines.

7 I took a coat (because of / because / reason) it was cold.

8 Small farms aren't as efficient (to / from / as) large farms.

9 Let me get this straight. You're (saying / telling / said) that you've found another job.

10 I want to know how much their salaries (are costing / costing are / do cost).

11 Would you like to have hot drinks (whatever / whoever / whenever) you want during the day?

12 If they (aren't / won't / don't) popular, we won't install them.

13 We asked for opinions (because / as a result / so that) we could please the majority of people.

14 His argument is (because / therefore / based on) feelings.

15 It was a nice day. (Contrast / However / Conclusion) we didn't go out.

16 It's not true, it's just a silly (talk / rumour / say).

17 OK, (let / let's / allow) me get this clear. You want more money.

18 When we paraphrase, we're saying the same thing in (a different / the same / a clever) way.

19 We use *because* when we are talking about (reasons / contrast / gossip).

20 *Because* is (an adjective / a noun / a link word).